A Short History of the Romanovs

The Rise and Fall of Russia's Most Famous Family

Stephen Collins

the information contained within this document, including, but not limited to, errors, omissions, or inaccuracies.

Table of Contents

Introduction

The Romanov family has long fascinated many people, from their personal stories to their integral input into the foundation of Russian Imperial history. Apart from this, their contribution to modern-day Russia is significant. The Romanovs were one of the lengthiest and most important dynasties in history, spanning over 300 years in Russian and world history. From the Middle Ages to the start of the modern era, the Romanov family seemed to have had more than their fair share of colorful characters and drama.

This book is a concise and easy-to-read historical summary that will take you through the rise and fall of this family's captivating tale, showing the human side of these powerful leaders. Fascinating stories unfold throughout this book of events that transpired through these years. Sometimes we may forget that this family, despite their enormous power, were people just like us fueled by both their strengths and weaknesses. The dynasty of the Romanovs is one of those stories that will be retold with different versions for the time to come as there were so many rumors and stories around almost every single thing they were involved in.

Weaving through these stories and the characters that formed the rise and fall of this dynasty provides a fascinating read. This book will deliver a solid understanding of important historical events and what transpired while bringing in the personalities of the leaders during that time.

Romanov History

There have been written accounts of these complex historical events, but what makes this book different is that it will provide a summary of the most important moments bringing in the complexity of this family without making it an overwhelming and a 'heavy' read. A great deal occurred during the period of their reign in history, and the key of this book is to provide a basic understanding of what transpired without leaving the important details out.

Focusing on those key anecdotes and happenings in their lives provides an entrancing journey into this period of history. The most prevalent story is the many murmurings of the rumored survival of some of the children from the brutal murders of Tsar Nicholas II, his wife Alexandra, and their five children by Bolshevik captors in Yekaterinburg on July 17, 1918. Even though it was proven in 2007 that these rumors were untrue, it still left some doubt and mystery. Nicholas II did not innately have what his predecessors had in terms of leadership skills—if anything he was an inadequate leader that ultimately made poor decisions and had little support from the Russian people. This paved the way for an uprising and the ultimate fall of Romanov rule when he was forced to abdicate amid World War I on June 15, 1917. This great moment in history placed his entire family under house arrest. It is believed by many historical researchers that Nicholas truly believed he was doing the right thing for Russia at the time and had little or no idea of the eventual and gruesome outcome for his treasured family.

Romanovs' Powerful Reign

Here is a synopsis of the Romanovs' powerful reign through the ages up until the Russian Revolution in 1917. The Romanov family had a pattern of succession during the first century of power, which generally passed the throne onto the tsar's eldest son or the closest eldest senior male relative, if there was no heir and son born into the family to assume the title. During this period some women did happen to come into power, which was a momentous and unusual occurrence to rule in this male-dominated society.

1613–1645: The first Romanov tsar and founder of the Romanov dynasty was Mikhail (or Michael) Fyodorovich Romanov. He was the son of Fyodor Nikitich Romanov and was related to the last tsar of the Rurik dynasty.

1645–1676: Mikhail Fyodorovich's son Alexis (Aleksey Mikhaylovich) succeeded his father upon death at the very young age of 16.

1676–1682: Fyodor III (Fyodor Alekseyevich), son of Alexis, ruled for only six years until his death when his brother Ivan V (Ivan V Alekseyevich) and his half-brother Peter I (Pyotr Alekseyevich Romanov), also known as Peter the Great, were both contenders for the throne. There was a massive dispute about who would rule and initially Peter I was appointed by the *zemsky sobor* (assembly of the land) as tsar, Ivan's supporters, the *streltsy* (military) coordinated a revolt upon the palace, which ultimately resulted in both Ivan and Peter taking the throne jointly for a period.

1682–1696: Ivan V shared the throne with Peter I during this period. When Ivan was severely incapacitated both physically and mentally, Peter I became the ultimate ruler between the pair until Ivan's death in 1696.

1682–1725: Peter the Great ruled Russia solely from 1696, and in his time, he abandoned the title of tsar and chose "emperor of all Russia" instead. He also instilled a new law of succession allowing monarchs a say in who would be their successor.

1725–1727: Upon Peter I's death, his wife Catherine (Yekaterina Alekseyevna) became empress by decree. This was most unusual during a time of male dominance and supremacy. She was a formidable woman who knew what she wanted and got it.

1727–1730: Upon Catherine's death, the throne fell back into "birth by blood" and Peter I's grandson, Peter II (Pyotr Alexeyevich Romanov), became emperor but only for a short period until his untimely death.

1730–1740: Without another male heir, Ivan V's daughter Anna (Anna Ivanovna Romanova) became empress until her death. Her great move was to revoke the Supreme Privy Council and reinstate the monarchy. Before her death, she appointed her great nephew Ivan VI (Ivan Antonovich) to be emperor though he was only an infant at the time.

1740–1741: Anna's niece and Ivan VI's mother, Anna Leopoldovna (Elisabeth Katharina Christine von

Mecklenburg-Schwerin) was named empress and placed as the regent for Ivan VI's rule.

1741–1761: The daughter of Peter I and Catherine I, Elizabeth (Yelizaveta Petrovna), staged a *coup d'etat* with the help of the French ambassador and other members of the Russian court to become empress. Her rule was significant in the re-establishment of some measures that her father had created, for example, removing the cabinet council system. She was integral in establishing Russia's first university in Moscow.

1762–1762: Elizabeth's nephew, Peter III, (Pyotr Fyodorovich), was proclaimed as heir to the throne in 1742 and was not popular nor of great mental capacity. His wife Catherine (Sophie von Anhalt-Zerbst), a German princess, conspired with the guard, the senate, and the church to overthrow her husband, Peter III. She became Catherine II and empress upon his abdication, and then he was murdered by one of the conspirators.

1762–1796: Catherine II ruled as empress and was referred to as Catherine the Great. She was the longest-reigning female ruler of her time. She was a patron of the arts and integral in implementing the restricted Russian law code.

1796–1801: Paul I (Pavel Petrovich), son of Catherine II and Peter III, was integral in the change of the succession law to create the order of succession to be back firmly in place for the Romanov family members.

1801–1825: Alexander I (Aleksandr Pavlovich) conspired to murder his father, Paul I, so he could become emperor. When Alexander I died, there was confusion about who would succeed him as the legitimate heir. His brother

Constantine covertly declined in favor of the brother Nicholas I (Nicolay Pavlovich).

1825–1855: Nicholas I was known as the emperor that "froze Russia for 30 years."

1855–1881: Alexander II (Aleksandr Nikolayevich), son of Nicholas I, had a liberal education and was dismayed at the result of the Crimean War that motivated him to instigate national changes in Russia, primarily the emancipation of the serfs in 1861. Revolutionary terrorism led to his assassination.

1881–1894: Alexander III (Aleksandr Aleksandrovich), the second son of Alexander II and Maria Aleksandrovna, was a strong supporter of nationalism and an adversary of a representative government. He founded schemes based on dictatorship and an Eastern Orthodox way of life. He had a strong belief in the Russian people to be one way and persecuted non-orthodox groups and minorities.

1894–1917: The last emperor of Russia, Nicholas II (Nikolay Aleksandrovich), was crowned tsar in Moscow on May 26, 1896 after succeeding his father. His family's brutal murder and the mystery that surrounded it have intrigued many.

This story will unravel some of the events, trials, and tribulations the Romanov family lived through and whose rule controlled aristocracy and altered history to form modern-day Russia.

Chapter 1:

Background to the Romanov

Dynasty

The Romanov family ruled for over three centuries from 1613 to 1917 and was the last imperial dynasty to rule Russia. Their dominance was quite remarkable with a revolution changing the path of their continued reign. The beginning of the Romanov bloodline is a bit vague, but it is strongly considered to begin with Andrei Ivanovich Kobyla back in the 14th century. He was a noble lord, and his line of descent split into quite a few directions over time, so it is difficult to establish a clear track of events. What is clear is that the five sons of Andrei ended up being relatives to numerous clans that included the Boborykins, Lodygins, Zherebtsovs, and many others.

It has been established that the Romanovs stem from the youngest son of Andrei Kobyla, Fyodor, who also was called "Koshka." This then became the Koshkir line and was also split up into a few different clans. When the grandson of Fyodor, Zakhary, died, the lineage became a bit clearer. He had two sons, Yakov and Yuri, who were well-known noblemen near the end of the 15th century. Yuri's family name became Yuriev, and his son was named Roman. It is gathered that this is where the Romanov name originated. Roman had a son called Nikita, who was a prominent *boyar*, or nobleman, at the time serving Ivan the Terrible from 1565. He was at the forefront of ceremonial events and functions at court and was also instrumental in the proceedings that followed the death of Ivan the Terrible in the regency council when Tsar Fyodor succeeded him. Roman also had a daughter called Anastasia who was married to Ivan the Terrible in 1547. This marriage not only catapulted the family into extreme privilege but also had the spoils of the power that came with it. It was also the foundation of the Yuriev descendants from Andrei Kobyla to eventually become the Romanovs.

The Romanovs assumed power shortly after the death of the first tsar, Ivan the Terrible, who was born on August 25, 1530 and died of a stroke on March 18, 1584. He was termed by this rather unfortunate title due to his extreme behavior during his reign. With supreme control of the power of military rule, he reigned terror upon the nobility to achieve his objectives. Ivan's main motivation against the nobility was to put limitations on the power of hereditary rights and to stop the dependence that they had on the tsar. He declared many wars that were both long and mostly unsuccessful against Sweden, Poland, and other countries.

Ivan married Anastasia Romanovna, who was great aunt to the very first tsar that began the tale of the Romanov dynasty. Ivan was a violent man and was thought to be unhinged in his behavior. There are many stories about his conduct, but the most significant one occurs in 1581 when he beat his son and heir to death in a bout of extreme rage. One wonders what rage can lead a father to kill his own flesh and blood. In addition to this, he was supposed to be the reason for his unborn grandson's unfortunate miscarriage due to the stress and horror of his mother experiencing her husband's death. This resulted in his younger son being the apparent heir to the throne. Fyodor Ivanovich was not a natural leader. This uncertainty led to what is known historically as the "Time of Troubles," which began in the late 1500s to around 1613 when the Romanov reign began. The "Time of Troubles" is viewed as a period of ultimate chaos and political crisis in Russia.

After the death of Ivan IV and Fyodor succeeding him, Boris Godunov was appointed to be his custodian as Fyodor was mentally incapable of ruling. This appointment gave Godunov supreme power being chief advisor to Tsar Fyodor between the period 1584-1598.

Upon Fyodor's death and with there being no apparent heir, Godunov became the self-appointed tsar of Russia for the period 1598 to 1605 when he was victorious in his defeat of the boyars, the privileged upper class and wealthy landowners who ultimately ruled Russia. The boyars had supreme power and were also advisors of the grand prince who was in power at the time. Who was to succeed Fyodor lay in the hands of the boyars who were also known as "the assembly of the land," a highly influential group of both the church and military. They were ranked by seniority and even though they were appointed by the princes as their advisors, their appointments were gauged on their ancestral importance. They held the highest ranks in the military, but more importantly, they maintained the right to leave the service of the prince without it affecting their wealth thus being able to retain their land and remaining very powerful.

For the next ten years, Russia suffered greatly with severe onslaughts from both the Poles and the Swedes that created chronic instability. Food shortages and mass uprisings prevailed. Godunov was not supportive of aristocratic systems as he was not royalty by blood but had risen through the ranks quite aggressively while he was in service to Ivan the Terrible. The marriage of his sister to the Tsar Fyodor cemented his position firmly among the elite. His privileged background and wealth allowed his massive power. If anyone came up against him while he ruled as acting tsar, they were immediately banished. His focus was purely on the further upliftment of the privileged. Gudunov did leave a legacy of being the first Russian ruler to permit education abroad and allowed the construction of the first Lutheran churches. With victory in the Russo-Swedish war that was fought between 1590 and 1595, he had his eyes on gaining power over Livonia with the benefit of a Baltic coastline being the prize. To bring royal blood into his family, he saw great merit in establishing good relations with the Scandinavian leader with perhaps a marriage between his family and theirs. Probably his most drastic reform was the implementation of the right of peasants not being allowed to exchange themselves between landowners. This was the groundwork of the establishment of the oppressive and long-lasting foundation of serfdom in Russia. He banished the Romanov family in an attempt to diminish the power of the boyars and aristocracy as he well knew that he was not the legitimate tsar. After Godunov died in 1605 from a stroke after suffering a long illness, there was a brief time when his son Fyodor II succeeded him. After only a few months, he was murdered by his family's enemies.

Romanov Reign Begins

In 1613, it was decided that Michael Romanov, the 16-year-old son of Fyodor Nikitich Romanov was to be appointed by the boyars as the tsar of Russia. Little did anyone know that he would effectively be one of the 18 future rulers in the Romanov dynasty for the next 300 years! Fyodor, also known as Filaret at the time of his son's appointment as tsar, was a prisoner of Poland. He was only to be released in 1619, and when he returned to Russia, father and son ruled together.

Apart from the legendary Ivan the Terrible, the most famous leaders during this period were Peter the Great, Catherine the Great, Alexander I, and Nicholas II. Here is a brief introduction to these famous Romanovs and more will be revealed in the chapters dedicated to them further in the book.

The Most Famous Romanovs

Peter the Great was a dedicated reformer taking Russia boldly forward with significant steps of power. At the beginning of his rule, Russia trailed far behind Western civilization, and through his initiatives, great leaps of advancement to catch up were implemented by him. Focus on the areas of development and the growth of the economy were affected by the progression of more trade and improved foreign policy. Sciences, culture, and educational standards were also key areas that were further developed during his rule.

Catherine the Great ruled Russia for 34 years, significantly longer than any other Russian female ruler. During her term of rule, she increased Russia's territory considerably. She was driven, determined, and refused to be overshadowed by her male counterparts. Her drive of integrating the cultural and political life of Europe into Russia was notable. Even today, many Russians continue to have a great sense of pride in her as being one of their past leaders.

Alexander I was integral in creating a turning point in Napoleonic history when his army defeated Napoleon's during its invasion of France in 1814. Alexander had a serious dislike for Napoleon, and this war was focused purely on defeating him and not necessarily the defeat of the French people. He built universities in Russia and was effective in instituting educational reforms.

Nicholas II was the last tsar to rule Russia under the Romanov name, which eventually, due to his poor leadership skills for the huge responsibilities he had, led to his abdication in 1917. He is viewed by many historians as a *well-meaning but indecisive leader.* Nicholas was greatly influenced by others and did not have the tenacity to understand what it was that Russia needed. He was easily manipulated and was not a good decision maker. He was unfortunate to place trust in and take advice from the incorrect people. This eventually led to a brutal execution of him and his family in 1918 that continues to be shrouded in mystery.

Going back to over 300 years ago when the Romanovs came into power, massive strides were made during their rule with the expansion of their territory. It is estimated that the Russian empire grew by 55 square miles (142 square kilometers) per day once the Romanovs came into power, ruling about one-sixth of the total area of the world in the late 19th century! It is as if the expansion of an empire was at the forefront of their thinking, and it was most certainly in their blood.

Russia's Progressive Transformation During Romanov Rule

Over the centuries of Romanov rule, the one thing that remained consistent was that serfs, who were essentially slaves, were doomed to be boxed into a continued status of the underclass of society with no chance of being able to change their status. This was only until the Emancipation Manifesto in 1861, which was proclaimed by Alexander II. This change was motivated by his understanding of the need to amend Russia's outdated policies to level the playing field regarding Western culture's acceptance of Russia. His bold move was not easily accepted by those that benefited greatly from this unbalanced class system, and it took many years to establish this change that was initiated in 1857. The process was slow and tedious for the peasants who were eventually allowed their freedom and were also promised land. So many restrictions were imposed with long periods of payments that they had to pay to the government for the land they were promised. The land in question was owned by their landlords and previous 'owners' of them when they were serfs, too. This whole process for them to pay for their land spanned 49 years! It was a futile attempt at giving the peasants what they wanted but also not actually giving them anything at all.

In 1881, and even after all this time, only about 85% of the peasants had received their promise of owning their very own piece of land. The massive surge in population growth added even more difficulties and created continued economic struggles. There was a small population of former serfs that did succeed in achieving some sort of progression, but they were few and far between with most remaining poor and with no land. It was only in 1905 these restrictive payments and conditions placed upon serfs in their quest to achieve ownership of land were lifted. By this stage, the loyalty by the serfs to their government that was aimed for with the Emancipation Manifesto had long since passed.

During the long reign of the Romanovs, it was clear their power was largely dominated by the immense control they had over a massive peasant population. This only changed with the uprising of these oppressed people, but not by very much, in the later years of their rule. When Peter I came into power, the most significant change he affected was his adaptation from a medieval to a more modern approach. The moves to empower the army and create a navy were prevalent in several ways. The transformations during his reign from connecting with European business and culture and creating progress in this regard made Peter I one of the forethinkers of his time. What is fascinating about what followed after Peter I's death in 1725 was the progression of women that came into power in a very male-dominated civilization. Peter I's daughter Elizabeth did not make a massive impact during her time of rule and was effective in continuing her rule in a similar way to her father's. She founded the first university in Moscow and the Academy of Arts in St. Petersburg. The ostentatious Winter Palace was also built during her time of rule.

Following Elizabeth was Catherine II who was influential in her vision of expansion of Russia to both the south and west. This impactful event coincided with the importance of establishing much-needed ports for trade on the Black Sea.

During the 19th century, Russia's compelling collection of tsars had either a reformist or reactionary way of ruling. Interestingly some had a bit of a mix of these two conflicting ways of ruling that came and left in waves during their over 300 years of power. It seems that the confusion between progress and staying as they were created much confusion over these numerous years. Contradictions of freedom and tyranny to the involvement of the lewd and mysterious, particularly during Alexander I's rule that clouded his great achievement in his defeat of Napoleon, added to the complexities of this family.

Nicholas I was undeniably dedicated to the monarchy and used dogmatic conventionalism of religion and 'Russification' (meaning to make even non-Russians Russian!) as his fundamental view on how to rule. Whereas when Alexander II came into power, his effect on the serfs had huge consequences both for the poor and the rich. He was termed "Tsar Liberator" and was committed to instilling his vision of change no matter the consequences. His progressive rule was put to a stop by revolutionaries that did not accept his vision. They had their own beliefs that they wanted to incorporate into what they thought was a liberation for Russians and ended Alexander II's rule by assassinating him.

When Alexander III stepped into power, his views were quite the opposite of his predecessor's to rule with more of an authoritarian stance. His view was that the people of Russia needed to be ruled "with an iron fist," so to speak. He wanted law and order and, thus, increased the oppression of his people once more. Nicholas II followed in the footsteps of his father with his ruling strategy focused on Russification and establishing Russia's foothold both nationally but also internationally. Nicholas II's rule is accepted to be the prelude to World War I after he failed to secure a victory in the Russo-Japanese War. In the years following 1917, Russia continued to be a militarized state that ultimately led to a revolution, bringing the Bolsheviks into power.

The end of the Romanov dynasty followed the abdication of Nicholas II and spearheaded the rise of the first Communist government in the world led by Vladimir Lenin. Sparked by the Russian Revolution in 1917 and fueled by destitute people who were low on food supplies, it was a desperate time for those living below the poverty line. Nicholas II's abdication meant his brother was supposed to take over the throne, but he was reluctant and that left the country reeling without a leader. The inequalities and total confusion when the State Duma took control didn't help matters. The State Duma was established in 1905 by Nicholas II and went through numerous changes to it during his reign, sometimes on a whim to suit his ideals. It was formed to split the opposition during an uprising and to allow the State Duma to control the enforcement of a law that was proposed. In other words, they had the final say at that time. The Duma consisted of a group of members ranging from 478 to 525 representatives of the country from landowners and farmworkers to middle-class workers and academics. Various formations of Dumas existed from the first one that was established and continue to exist today with various changes to their powers and roles they played.

Chapter 2:

Peter the Great

There are many memorial statues featured all over St. Petersburg, where Peter the Great is revered as the founder of the city. His remains lie in the Cathedral of St. Paul and St. Peter, which overlooks a massive bronze sculpture in St. Petersburg that stands proudly depicting him as a hero and honored leader. Peter was born in Moscow on May 30, 1672 and died in St. Petersburg on February 8, 1725. It is thought that he succumbed from an infection of his bladder.

Peter ruled Russia for 42 years, and during this time, he founded St. Petersburg in 1703 following the battle with Sweden, creating accessibility to the Baltic Sea. Peter made St. Petersburg the capital of Russia in 1712, bumping Moscow off this coveted title. Even though Moscow again became the capital, St. Petersburg is often referred to as the cultural capital.

During his reign, and incorporating the German influence he had growing up, Peter the Great chose St. Petersburg to be the city where he could build something Russia did not have. He used experience gained from Europe and brought architects to construct buildings that were unlike any others in Russia. This city attracted foreigners and the aristocracy. It became a hub for education, arts, and culture, which was his ultimate dream. He was the youngest son of Alexey I and his second wife Natalya Naryshkina. Peter took over the throne from his elder half-brother Fyodor III, who was disabled and only ruled for a short period of six years. Peter was tutored as other tsars before him by palace tutors but additionally by tutors in Germantown that was a region of Moscow where sophisticated educators and foreigners lived. His passion for the sciences and the development of technology was inspired by these tutors. This was unusual for Russian tsars to be interested in this 'new' information rather than learning about the existing, and somewhat outdated, educational practices.

Peter I was tsar from 1682 when he was only 10 years old and co-reigned with his half-brother Ivan from 1682 until 1696. It was a brutal time he lived through as a young boy as Ivan's sister Sophia Alekseyevna's relatives were adamant that she should rule. Ivan was severely incapacitated, suffering from both physical and psychological issues. Many of Peter's family members were killed during this tumultuous time of riots and violence, which some historians consider may have been the foundation of his sometimes harsh but fiercely determined behaviors in his adulthood. Eventually, it was decided that Sophia was to be regent and that Ivan, who became Ivan V, would share the throne with Peter.

Peter remained in the village of Preobrazhenskoye with his mother until he turned 17, only attending important ceremonies in Moscow when he needed to. His mother was influential in his upbringing and in preparing him to be a ruler. It was during this time of his childhood that he realized his passion for sailing.

In 1689, Peter was only 17 years of age when he was victorious in removing Sophia from power, but it was only in 1696 that he became a full-fledged tsar after the death of Ivan V on February 8. Despite the brutality of his autocratic way of ruling, he was powerful in transforming Russia into a power that was known worldwide, making him one of the greatest rulers of all time.

At the age of 24, Peter traveled to Europe incognito as Pyotr Mikhailov to find allies and further his quest for knowledge and skills from Western culture. Peter was fascinated with carpentry and learnt about the art of building ships while experiencing the workings of dockyards in Holland. He also received his certification in firearms in Prussia and ended up in England where he furthered his studies focused on the maritime industry. While in London, he had the opportunity to listen to the proceedings of the House of Commons that were said to horrify him at how commoners could dare to object in public to their rulers. Peter continued his educational travels around Europe learning about the Western culture for a total of about 18 months when he had to return to Russia due to a streltsy, or military, revolt in Moscow. The knowledge and intrigue he had with the West are depicted in the decor of his palaces, his personal collections, and his library. Peter receiving an education both in Russia and overseas was a first for a Russian monarch.

Peter married Eudoxia Lopukhina and had three children with her, but their marriage arranged by his mother was not a happy one, ending in divorce in 1712. Eudoxia was forcibly made to live in a convent at the same time Peter married Marta Skavronskaya, who ended up becoming Catherine I and empress of Russia. Interestingly, Marta was a servant to his friend Alexander Menshikov and was at first his mistress. Upon her marriage, her name was changed to Catherine. Their marriage was a happy and passionate one with 11 children. Unfortunately, only two girls lived to be adults resulting in no male heir.

So What Made Peter Great?

Ascending to the throne near the end of the 17th century, Peter the Great found himself ruler of a Russia that was far removed from European politics. Steeped in superstitious behavior, an innate belief in conservatism, and unwavering distrust of non-Russians, this was a society out of date and out of touch with the rest of the world. Peter's drive was to make Russia great and to catch up with Westernization through his authoritarian forcing of Western policies upon his people. Trade, education, science, architecture, and culture were all included in his quest to Westernize his people. Even releasing Russia's first newspaper on January 13, 1703 was one of his bold initiatives for this period. Peter believed that the public should be informed about what was happening in their country and beyond. He didn't seem to take into account that most Russians were illiterate at that time.

When he brought potatoes and sunflowers back from his travels in Holland, he was under the impression that the people would welcome these staple food items. What he failed to do was send instructions with these items of how to prepare them. Never mind his people being resistant to change, too. Potatoes were for some time called "Devil's apple" as people tried to eat the leaves, not understanding that it was the tuber underground that was the edible part.

Unfortunately, the leaves were poisonous and caused many deaths! Eventually, the information was distributed to the people, and potatoes became a staple diet for Russians by the turn of the 19th century. The sunflower was a bit easier for the peasants to work out from the beginning using the seeds and making oil.

Before Peter came into power, the peasants were taxed per household and not per person, so Peter devised the very first census to work out how many males there were in each household and that each male had to pay 70 kopeks. Without the census, there was no way of knowing if the government was being short-changed. Peter increased the peasant's taxes substantially by doing this. According to census records captured, there were about 12 million people living in Russia at the time.

His notable accomplishments apart from the founding of St. Petersburg were his victorious defeat of Sweden in 1703 in the Battle of Poltava and his creation of the Russian navy, which became a major maritime power. He also formed an army and instituted conscription for every citizen no matter their social status. Apart from an army or navy of Russians, he also recruited foreigners that were experts in their field to serve. This was the beginning of the next two centuries of Russia recruiting professionals from abroad. Peter established the Table of Ranks in both the army and the navy, which was split into 14 levels. This was primarily to create a platform from which those who deserved recognition for hard work were able to rise up in the ranks.

The expansion of Russian borders during Peter's rule led to notable cultural and political change. The integration of Westernized systems and bringing in modernization with the view to end the dominance of conservatism and religion in Russia was envisaged by him. Moving his people towards a more modern Russia was truly a great achievement and earned him the name he was dubbed.

He introduced extraordinarily high taxes, had violent outbursts, led several revolts, suppressed any rebellion, and had some strange ideas, such as a beard tax on men who dared to adorn a beard! He wanted his fellow men to dress in European fashion and be clean-shaven. He had no qualms about sending intelligent young noblemen overseas for further education at the state's expense, and he was personally invested in monitoring their progress.

His decision to change the calendar from the old Russian calendar to the Julian calendar to start the calendar years from the birth of Christ created huge opposition from the Russian Orthodox Church. This momentous event took place on January 1, 1700, using the method of Christianity counting dates from the birth of Christ. The Russian calendar started on September 1 using the Byzantine practice of noting the birth of Adam. This was a drastic change as one day Russia was in 7208 and the next in 1700. Peter determined this change was integral to Russia and to keep up with Europe.

The Julian calendar was devised in ancient Rome when Julius Caesar ruled. This calendar year was figured out by calculating the number of days between the two spring equinoxes, which came to a total of 362.25 days. It was only in the 14th century that the error in counting the days was discovered. Using the old Russian calendar also meant that Christian Easter and Jewish Passover would not ever fall on the same days. This is more than likely the reason why the Russian Orthodox Church objected so fiercely to the change as these celebrations were not permitted to be worshiped concurrently. When Peter affected this dramatic change, he also enforced various celebrations lasting a week long. Decorations with the branches from trees like pine, juniper, and fir were to be used to adorn houses and the neighborhood. His bold move meant that various other religious occasions were misplaced due to the changes in the calendar that did not fare well with the church. As a side note, taking us many years later to 1918 after the revolution, the Bolsheviks also made a change to the calendar. The Julian calendar that was being followed was 13 days behind the Westernized Gregorian calendar. This change was made to "catch up" and was viewed by the Bolsheviks as yet another way Russia had fallen behind the times and not taken into account the leap years. It was also another dismissal of the tsarist regime. Today Russia celebrates two New Year's celebrations, one on January 1 as the rest of the world does and the other on January 14, called "Old New Year" to acknowledge the "old Russia" Peter the Great had influenced.

There are stories of Peter enjoying the entertainment of drunken dwarfs and others and of his own excessive drinking, plus the expectation of those to drink as much as he did. He would have violent outbursts of temper exploding at those that dared to cross him. He also portrayed dark behavior such as beheading a previous mistress and then detailing the anatomy of the throat when holding her decapitated head in his hands! It was almost as if he had two opposite personalities—a statuesque, intelligent figure that had no fear of hard work and expected the same of his counterparts or else suffer the wrath of his terrible dark side that could lead to violent and demented behavior.

The Mystery of the Death of Alexei

However, Peter the Great was also known to be a tyrant, and probably one of the most famous stories about him was the ordering of the torture of his eldest son, Alexei, which ultimately resulted in his death. Peter thought that his son, who had very different views from his father, was conspiring against him, and this led to a dramatic turn in 1718. The relationship began to sour between father and son when Alexei's mother was confined to a convent after the divorce when he was only eight years old, leaving him to be raised by his aunts. He received an excellent education by order of his father, but they did not see much of each other as he was growing up. Alexei was surrounded by those who still had the old-fashioned way of thinking of Russia, and he often avoided spending time with his father, feigning illness and not even attending the wedding of Peter and Catherine. He even went as far as to injure his hand purposefully rather than attend one of his father's requirements.

Alexei had an unhappy marriage that was arranged by Peter and that ended with his wife dying after complications after the birth of their second child. He was admonished by his father constantly, and their relationship continued to fail with Peter reaching the end of his tether with his son's inability to reach his expectations. Peter penned a letter to his son in 1715, stating his displeasure at his lack of military expertise with threats of denying him the succession to the throne. It was a bitter and nasty letter outlining his disappointment with his son. Alexei's response to all this was to agree with his father and even relinquish the throne, but this still did not satisfy Peter as he expected his son to show him that he did have the personality and strength to stand up for himself and become a powerful ruler. An ultimatum was given to Alexei by his disappointed father to either attend a monastery to become a monk or strive to be fit to achieve a succession to the throne. The option of becoming a monk was chosen by Alexei, but instead of doing this, he escaped Russia and ended up in Austria seeking refuge with Emperor Charles VI. Peter's concerns about his son and his fear of him conspiring against him were fueled by Alexei's association and relationships with the old-fashioned aristocracy and the bureaucratic elite, who were not fans of Peter's way of ruling Russia. In 1717 Peter's guards managed to hunt down Alexei in hiding where he was presented with a letter from his father with promises of no punishment if he returned to Russia. Alexei decided to return. Little did he know that he would be forced to beg for forgiveness publicly, which resulted in extreme measures of punishment and torture, even the execution of the individuals who helped him escape after his father demanded their names from him. His mother was also punished by banishing her to an even more remote convent. This was not the end of Peter's wrath upon his son as he was convinced his son must have been conspiring against him. The sad tale ended up with Alexei being tortured until his apparent confession of conspiring against his father. It is not certain exactly how he died, but it is assumed the arduous and continued torture ordered by his father in the Fortress of Peter and Paul resulted in his unseemly death. The circumstances of his death continue to be shrouded in mystery and blurry with detail to today.

Even though during these times it was common to hear about bloody feuds among royalty, this instance of the cruelty of a father upon his own son cannot be measured against any other.

Although some of his methods leaned toward the more extreme side, or even beyond that to sheer lunacy, Peter is still respected today as a progressive thinker who was fearless and led Russia toward a more modern approach. Some historians believe that his reforms were the leading point in forming Russia into the superpower that it became.

Chapter 3:

Catherine the Great

Catherine the Great, who was the longest-reigning female ruler in Russia, was born in Poland on May 2, 1729 as Sophie von Anhalt-Zerbst, daughter of a penniless Prussian prince. She died as an empress, known as Catherine the Great, on November 17, 1796. Her reign of 34 years was not only colorful with her escapades but also effective in the significant expansion of Russian territory under her rule and the shuffling of Russian laws. Catherine still remains respected by many Russians today as a strong feminist role model. Her period of rule is often referred to as the Golden Age of the Russian Empire as it grew significantly from strength to strength during this time.

At the tender age of 16, she married Karl Ulrich, who later became Peter III and was heir to the throne. This arranged marriage was not a happy union. Peter III was grossly incompetent as a leader, which ultimately resulted in Catherine seizing her opportunity to lead. She grew frustrated with her husband's childish obsessions and apparent disregard for his duties. Her successful revolt against her husband in cahoots with her lover, Grigory Grigoryevich, Count Orlov, led to his abdication, and in 1762, she became empress of Russia. This move for power was motivated when Peter III was on holiday allowing Catherine to meet with the military and conspire for them to protect her. Orlov was a lieutenant, and this certainly helped convince the military to arrest Peter III upon his return. After only six months on the throne, he was forced to abdicate, but it did not go so smoothly. Orlov's younger brother Alexei strangled Peter III to death under mysterious circumstances that were not, according to most, the intention or plan that Catherine had in mind.

What may have seemed like a coup that had ulterior motives for the lovers, Catherine and Orlov, did not turn out to have a love story ending. Catherine met a man during this tumultuous time called Grigory Potemkin, who served in the guard that arrested Peter III. Their relationship was a solid one that blossomed in their mutual interests and, of course, passion for each other. Potemkin was known for efforts in the Russo-Turkish War, and they also made a formidable team to seize Crimea and develop the Russian Black Sea naval fleet.

So What Made Catherine Great?

She was a woman that was to be admired and one that deserved the title to her name of "The Great." She arrived in Russia as a young German girl, driven by fierce independence, intelligence, and charm, who wanted to be completely and totally loved by another but was sorely disappointed in her chosen husband. This was the foundation that led to her determination to take over and rule herself, and this is what she succeeded in doing.

Catherine was a very powerful woman and was known for her contradictory nature and sanctimonious militarist views. She was also a brave and passionate woman who ruled under a shadow of entangled misinterpretation of who she really was. Her marriage to Peter III, which was horribly unhappy due to their obvious incompatibility, was the start of her own uprising within herself. Catherine came from a background of European culture and excitement, and this is probably part of what led her to seek excitement elsewhere from her boring marriage. There are even rumors that the child they had together, Paul, was not actually Peter's and was the child of her early lover Sergei Saltykov. Her sexual exploits were well-known. She was educated and was motivated to expand her knowledge, and when Peter III became tsar, she was almost forced into an isolated life that was not at all in her destiny. She spent a great deal of time furthering her education and learning about the workings of the government and becoming knowledgeable in a number of other subjects. She soon came to the realization that she could do a far better job than her husband.

Her drive to make changes in all spheres of governing was quite remarkable, ranging from administration to medical intervention where she was a proponent of the smallpox vaccine in 1768, receiving it herself.

Her interests in philosophy were prevalent in her communications with the French philosopher Voltaire, and she inspired many Russians during her rule to embrace a European way of life. An avid supporter of the arts, she saw the Hermitage Museum open that housed part of her personal art collection. Female artists flourished under her time of rule, and those that were academically inclined had more opportunities to engage in furthering their studies.

"The Great" moniker was another title that she was known by, and during her rule from 1762 to 1796, she advocated for Enlightenment ideals and steered the government in

1766 to draw up a new bill of law for Russia called the *Nakaz*. She created this document drawing from the influence of Montesquieu, Rousseau, and other Enlightenment intellectuals that disapproved of torture and the death penalty by the government. She was famous for the creation of this political document, *Instruction of Catherine the Great,* which was a newly written law intended to reform her government and was positioned around liberal philanthropic political ideals. Even though Russia did not completely embrace the *Nakaz,* it was very significant in showing Russia where her principles lay.

The instructions were:

- All men should be considered equal before the law.

- The law should protect, not oppress, the people.

- The law should only forbid harmful acts.

- Serfdom should be abolished.

- Capital punishment and torture should cease.

- The principle of absolutism should be upheld.

Apart from these achievements, she was effective in expanding Russia's borders while the country was in a strong position in Eastern Europe. Catherine encountered many rebellions during her reign that made her even stronger and more formidable as a leader. Facing so many uprisings during her reign led her to appoint people that she trusted into positions of power, such as placing one of her lovers, Stanislaw Poniatowski, onto the Polish throne when the Polish king Augustus III died in 1763. Polish Catholics were unhappy with her insistence on giving power to Poland's Orthodox and Protestant followers. When Russian troops entered Poland, they were faced with a rebellion of Polish Catholics that created much turmoil.

Turkey also began to rise up against Russia, which ultimately led to a declaration of war in 1768. Russia under Catherine's rule defeated Turkey with relative ease and ended up with an expansion of territory on the Black Sea coast and the Sea of Azov.

The issue of serfdom and slavery was a huge thorn in her side. It was probably the reason why some referred to her as a hypocritical aristocrat as she made huge moves to abolish this due to her Enlightenment ideals. Serfdom continued long after Catherine's reign and only ended in 1861 when Alexander II implemented the Emancipation Manifesto. However, in reality, it continued for many more years as the upper societies were not sold on the idea completely. These downtrodden people lived in appalling conditions and had the hardest jobs working in mines and factories, and it was known that not many of them lived past middle age. Even if Catherine personally felt that it was wrong, there was not much she could do about it in reality without unsettling her seat of power and the support of the elite.

A decree was published by the government in 1767 with part of it stating:

> *And should it so happen that even after the publication of the present decree of Her Imperial Majesty and serfs and peasants should cease to give the proper obedience to their landlords…and should make bold to submit unlawful*

petitions complaining of their landlords, and especially to petition Her Imperial Majesty personally, then both those who make the complaints and those who write up the petitions shall be punished by the knout (whip) and forthwith deported to Nerchinsk to penal servitude for life. (Jarus, 2017).

This massive divide between the elite and the poor came to a head upon Russia's entry into World War I when the military was under pressure and living conditions worsened for the poor. This was also the end of the era of Romanov rule and civil war erupted.

During Catherine's reign in 1773, she experienced the emergence of Yemelyan Pugachev, who not only organized a rebellion against her but also alleged to be her executed husband, Peter III. This was untrue and unfounded, and his motivation was to stir up the masses for support. He had great support from the serfs and poor people of Russia, giving speeches about releasing them from tax, easing their financial woes, offering them land that they would own that would be taken from the nobles and the like. His uprising did not last long, as he was soon captured and executed.

The Many Loves of Catherine's Life

Catherine was known to be voracious in her love life escapades! She penned the words, to her lover Potemkin in her Sincere Confession of February 21, 1774, "The trouble is that my heart is loathe to remain even one hour without love" (Kelly, 2006).

Many viewed her as promiscuous, but the truth was although she had many lovers, she remained true and faithful to those she had a relationship with, except for her husband Peter. There are stories flung around that none of the children that were born during their marriage were biologically his. Sergei Saltykov is thought to be the father of at least Paul I, who succeeded her, and perhaps even the father of more of her other children. Stanislaus Poniatowski was believed to be the father of one of her daughters, and Grigory Orlov is believed to be the biological father of one of her sons. Catherine was known to be extremely generous to her ex-lovers and presented them with many gifts. It seems she had a sensitive heart and loved deeply.

In today's terms, Catherine probably would have been viewed as a "party animal," but she set limits to her partying time. A famous decree by her was "no ladies are to get drunk upon any pretense whatever nor shall gentlemen before 9 p.m." Her sense of humor was evident!

Grigory Potemkin was known to be the great love of her life. They met on the day of the coup to overthrow her husband, Peter III in 1762. He was relatively younger than her, 10 years her junior at the age of 24. They began their love affair that lasted only two years with the agreement of what would be considered today an open relationship. He would be involved in choosing her lover for when he was away traveling. He fully understood that although she was capable of ruling on her own, she could not be physically on her own. She even chose some companions for him, too, and it was believed that not all these relationships they had with other people were sexual. They both seemed to not like to be alone.

There were some rumors of Grigory and Catherine being married in secret, but these are unfounded. Catherine would not marry another as this would mean splitting power, and it could affect her status greatly, which she did not want changed. This did not deter the love they felt for each other, which was clear in the many letters they exchanged over the years. When the passion for each other faded, this did not affect their friendship and love for one another with Catherine being completely devastated upon hearing of Grigory's death in 1791. Grigory was hugely influential in the ruling of Russia by her side as a partner but not as a full-fledged tsar.

Later Catherine had many lovers that were much younger than her, and this caused much discussion and judgment among her peers. Even though she had the reputation of being a seductive temptress with strings of lovers, she was quite reserved and did not tolerate crude jokes. Nudity remained strictly in the arts, too! She was a hard worker and rose to make her own coffee in the morning, which was quite unusual for a woman of her status.

Her need for companionship was clouded as being a sexual deviant by some, but this mostly came from those who did not support her and hoped to weaken her status as a powerful ruler.

Catherine's Death and Her Successor

After Catherine died in 1796, her adversaries created a number of disgusting stories including that her death was due to a sexual act with a horse or that she died while on a toilet. Both are far from the truth. They are a poor reflection on what this incredible woman actually did for Russia.

She suffered a stroke when she was 67 on November 16, 1796 and fell into a deep coma and succumbed the following day. Her son Paul I was the next in line of succession to rule the Russian empire. Paul did not rule for very long and was assassinated on March 23, 1801 by a group of traitors who not only forced him to abdicate but violently strangled and stomped upon him until he died. The event was covered up with a story that he had died of a stroke, but his injuries were so severe that most of his body had to be covered up when it was placed in the coffin for viewing.

Even though it was rumored that Paul was not the biological son of Catherine's husband, the Grand Duke Peter Fyodorovich, he was recognized by him as his son. What is interesting is that if he was indeed not the biological son, then all future Romanovs would not genetically have been Romanovs either! Paul did not have a good relationship with his mother, which was partly due to the fact that they did not see each other from his birth until he was eight years old. Paul spent his early years with his great-aunt Elizabeth. It was only after Peter III's death that Paul came to live with his mother, but their relationship was strained. Paul's first wife died in childbirth and so did their son. In a matter of months, Paul married again and proceeded to have ten children with his second wife, Maria Fyodorovna. His eldest son, Alexander, succeeded him, and even though he was informed about the coup to force his father to abdicate, he was unaware that it would result in his father's death.

Synopsis of Successors After Catherine the Great Until Nicholas II

The Romanov empire was firmly back on track when Paul I came into power, followed by his son Alexander. When Alexander died in 1825 of typhus, there was a flurry of confusion about who would reign next as both of his daughters had died as young children. First, Alexander's brother Constantine, who was in Poland as a commander for the Russian army declined, but this is shrouded in some mystery as he declined in secret, so the reasons why are not exactly clear. The secrecy was upon the order of Alexander so had to be followed through. One of the interesting theories is that because he was married to a Polish woman, Joanna Grudzińska, who had not descended from any royal blood this would have denied any of their children being able to succeed their father. Constantine's declining the throne threw some doubt over why Nicholas I should take his place and stirred up more conspiracy in the Romanov's captivating tale of successions. Nicholas was unaware of the secrecy of Constantine's abdication and assumed his brother was coming to take his rightful position, even swearing allegiance to him.

Nicholas would take the throne under some duress, and his first order of business was to suppress an uprising by noblemen against his appointment. The Decembrist Revolt was firmly and swiftly squashed by the newly crowned Tsar Nicholas I, who ruled Russia until 1855. He was commonly known as the emperor that "froze Russia for 30 years." He was not like any of his predecessors who welcomed industrialization and improvement, so he effectively slowed any progress in this form as much as he could during his reign. Granted he had a dramatic start, so perhaps, this was the determining factor of his harsh and brutal ruling technique. He was a staunch military man and ruled with an iron fist with high expectations of those that served him and those that he ruled over. He was a traditionalist and did not put up with any form of protest or disobedience. He also put a stop to education overseas and raised tuition fees in Russia to be unaffordable for most. When it came to serfdom, he was thought to think it evil but did little to alleviate the problems facing the downtrodden peasants. He was totally committed to everything Russian and did not want any European influence, but this was already spreading throughout the country, and the arts flourished even under his dogmatic reign.

As a child, Alexander II, who was next in line for the throne as the eldest son of Nicholas I, was somewhat overshadowed by his controlling father. He focused on his studies and was fortunate to have the support of his mother to receive his liberal education. During his reign from 1855 to 1881, he was effective in dragging Russia back from the change many sought and was effective in his attempt to bring Russia back into line with Western civilization. He was known as the "Tsar Liberator" mostly because he finally was the one to eradicate serfdom in 1861. For the first time, Russia had a judicial system in place by the Statute of 1864 that he implemented. In 1874, conscription was enforced upon all young men from the age of 20 and from all classes being ordered to serve in the military for a period of six years full-time followed by nine years as reservists. His acceptance of Westernization was not welcomed by all, and even though he was liberally minded, he was still a strong supporter of autocracy. There were multiple attempts to murder him, and he managed to dodge six of these attempts to assassinate him. Eventually, in

March 1881, the terrorist revolutionary organization The People's Will was successful in killing him in a horrific bomb attack in St. Petersburg.

Alexander III, father of Nicholas II, became tsar after his father's assassination from 1881 to 1894. An orthodox way of life was important to him, and he strongly believed in nationalism. He was not interested in a government that was representative, and he ruled by a dictatorship firmly committed to all things Russian. He was more akin to his grandfather's ways than his father. He was not initially first in line to the throne as this was meant to pass to his elder brother Nikolay, who had died in 1865. On Nikolay's deathbed, his wish was that his brother should marry his fiancèe, Maria Fyodorovna, and fortunately for both of them, this was a happy marriage. Only when it was apparent that he was to be tsar, did Alexander III then plunge himself into studying the intricacies of how he was going to rule Russia. He was greatly influenced and had his thoughts shaped by the political philosopher K.P. Pobedonostsev. Alexander and his father bumped heads many times with their differences over the years until his death. Alexander wasted no time in changing any of the liberal policies that his father had implemented. His view was simply guided by three values he intended on upholding: orthodoxy, autocracy, and national principle. One nation, one language, one religion, and one government was his goal. Persecution of minorities and non-orthodox groups was rife under his rule.

Chapter 4:

Nicholas II Becomes the Last Tsar

Nicholas II, who was to be the very last tsar of Russia, is also thought to have been the most inadequate leader Russia ever had. He never wanted to be a leader, certainly not as early as he found himself landed in the role. In some ways, his privileged upbringing was the downfall of his comprehension of what it was that the Russian people needed and expected in a leader. He also did not have the natural disposition of someone who was respected as a leader. Despite his reluctance of becoming a leader earlier than he expected, he did wholly believe that he was fully entitled due to his heritage and autocracy. His nature was shy, and he did not feel comfortable with all the pomp and ceremony befitting of the expectations of a tsar. His manner could be considered childish as he was quite envious of his ministers' aptitude to be decisive leaders, even bordering on jealousy. His manner created much distrust among those that were meant to be his most trusted confidants. Nicholas was born in Russia on May 18, 1868 and died violently on July 17, 1918.

Background

Nicholas II was the eldest son of Alexander III and his wife Maria Fyodorovna (Dagmar of Denmark) and the designated heir. Nicholas had and unfortunate and traumatic experienced of having witnessed his grandfather, Alexander II's, assassination attempt by bombing in St. Petersburg. This marked another turning point in Russian history.

The revolutionary group that was responsible for the assassination attempt was formed in 1879 and was called Narodnaya Volya, or the People's Will. They were driven by their determination to halt autocratic rule over Russia. They were of the mystic view that getting rid of the tsar and toppling "the man at the top" would thereby create such a drastic change of events it would end autocratic rule. The peasants would then rise up, and a new order would be formed. Multiple attempts were made by this group upon Alexander II's life finally leading to his death on March 13, 1881.

The bombing was a brutal attack and resulted in him losing his legs and being seriously injured before succumbing to his death. Despite witnessing this traumatizing event, Nicholas had a simple and happy childhood.

Alexander III was a tough and extremely forceful man who was huge in stature and had repressive behavior. His focus was on autocracy, and he was known to have viewed his father's rule as too lenient. The People's Will group that was responsible for his father's death was immediately hunted down, arrested, and suppressed. The assassins were hanged. One of these assassins, Alexander Ulyanov (known to his family as Sasha) was the elder brother of Vladimir Lenin. Ulyanov was absolutely committed to his cause and refused to beg for forgiveness other than seeking mercy for his mother who would be severely affected by his death. This fell upon deaf ears, and he was hanged shortly thereafter. Lenin was 17 years old at the time and studying law at Kazan University, and this event would be the leading step in the ultimate death of Nicholas II and his family ending the Romanov empire of rule.

Alexander III never declared war upon another country during his reign even though he was a powerful leader with competent advisers. He knew that Russia was an undeveloped state and needed to expand its industrialization infrastructure. It was also way behind Western power when it came to its defensive forces. His dictatorship rule was strict and severe with a view that if no weakness or division was seen upon his rule, it would be safe from uprising or revolts against it. During this continued autocratic rule, despite the obvious rebellion against it from groups such as the People's Will, the middle classes were denied any opinion of political expression. However, a wave of oppression was mounting against the tsar and the aristocracy.

Nicholas received education from private tutors covering the arts, history, languages, the sciences to even dancing and acquiring horsemanship and shooting skills. However, nothing prepared him for becoming a tsar. His father was under the illusion he would rule for many years and that there was ample time to educate his son on how to rule Russia befitting a tsar. Nicholas had a carefree life and very few responsibilities.

As young men, Nicholas and his brother George departed on a royal tour to visit Japan, China, India, and the Middle East in 1891. Near the end of their trip to Japan, while traveling through Otsu and on their way to Kyoto to greet the Emperor, there was an assassination attempt on Nicholas. Ironically it was a policeman who was assigned to protect him from the crowds that tried to strike at his head with a sword. The man, Tsuda Sanzo, made his way to the rickshaw Nicholas was traveling in and struck at his head with his sharp sword. The injury Nicholas received was quite a severe gash and was the cause of persistent headaches he suffered for many years afterward. Tsuda was promptly captured, and it was subsequently discovered at his trial that he thought Nicholas was a spy from Russia although this was broadly thought of as a false story. There were a few theories on why he attempted to kill Nicholas, but none were confirmed as the final story of exactly why. Tsuda was sentenced to life imprisonment in 1891 and died the same year. Speculation that he was poisoned ran rife, but there was no proof of it.

There were factors among the Japanese that were quite suspicious of the Russian entourage before this incident, and some thought they were, in fact, there to spy on Japan. The majority were fearful of the vengeance that may transpire from this attack on Nicholas. Emperor Meiji issued a public apology, and many Japanese citizens sent telegrams of good wishes for his recovery. A woman named Yuko Hatakeyama even was believed to have slit her throat as a drastic declaration of apologizing for the attacker's cruel act on the prince! Upon being informed of the unfortunate incident regarding an attack on his son's life, Alexander III ordered their immediate return home.

Even though Nicholas handled the attack very well and almost seemed a bit nonchalant about it all, this incident may have led to Nicholas's distrust and prejudice of the Japanese people. He had the thought the Japanese were inferior to the Russians and could be conquered with ease.

Not much time went by until Nicholas's marriage to Alexandra (Aleksandra Fyodorovna), a princess from Germany, granddaughter of Queen Victoria, and Grand Duke Louis IV's daughter. It was a happy one. They met when he was 16 and she was 12, and he knew then that this was whom he wanted to marry one day. When he first proposed, she did not accept because by marrying a Russian tsar, she would need to convert from Lutheran to Russian Orthodox faith, but eventually she ended up doing so.

Early in their engagement, Alexander III became very ill quite suddenly and finally succumbed to nephritis, which is an inflammation of the kidneys, on November 1, 1894. Nicholas was devastated at the loss of his father and now had the pressure of becoming tsar to face at the same time. All this happened much earlier than anyone expected.

Russia was deeply steeped in oppression and radical behavior and was far behind Western culture. Right from the start of Nicholas's rule, Russia was in turmoil, and he was ill-prepared to lead. He was a true autocrat and had never received any preparations on how to become tsar. He also did not have any understanding of the desperate quandary his people were in. A significant moment was when he was crowned tsar in 1896. A massive crowd of people assembled on the Khodynka Field in Moscow, where they were to be given coronation gifts and mementos, but it ended in a bloody devastating tragedy. A stampede occurred, crushing 1,400 people to death, which in turn led to his nickname being coined—"Nicholas the Bloody." In spite of this horrific event, Nicholas and his family continued to proceed with the celebrations and parties in honor of his tsardom. The Russian people were shocked as it seemed as if he did not care in the least that so many of his people had just died. It was almost as if he was doomed from the start.

In 1904, Nicholas and Alexandra, who had four daughters already—Olga, Tatiana, Maria, and Anastasia—finally had a son, Alexei. But this momentous event soon was clouded by the discovery that he suffered from hemophilia. This life-threatening and debilitating genetic disease is passed down from parents to children and essentially is the absence of blood being able to clot, resulting in chronic and unstoppable bleeding that can be fatal. It also presents itself with unbearable suffering if a bruise is formed from a bump or a fall, which results in internal bleeding and excruciating pain.

Women who carry the hemophilia genes can pass it along unwittingly to their children by either being a carrier or suffering from hemophilia. Research today is, of course, far more advanced than what it was in 1904, and what is dreadfully sad is that the type of hemophilia Alexei suffered from could have been managed and treated in modern times. The type of hemophilia he suffered from was discovered in 2007 when extensive genetic testing was done upon the remains of the Romanov children. Another interesting discovery is that although the family lived under a cloud of doom that hemophilia was being spread by their daughters into other families, which resulted in the older two girls never marrying, it was only Anastasia who carried the gene. One wonders where the two older girls would have ended up if they had indeed married. Incidentally, fathers who carry the gene cannot pass it along due to the make-up of chromosomes in males and females. Alexandra carried this gene that was unwittingly passed down from her mother, Princess Alice, and her grandmother, Queen Victoria of Great Britain. Alexandra's sister Irene, who was married to the prince of Prussia gave birth to two sons that both were hemophiliacs, and sadly, they died at a very young age. One can only imagine the undue stress Alexandra was put under once it was realized Alexei had it.

Nicholas the Family Man and the Introduction of Rasputin

Once Alexei had been born and the realization of his illness was confirmed by the persistent bleeding from his navel shortly after birth, the family was devastated. Never mind the worry about his health, the consequences of the heir to the throne being in any way incapacitated wreaked havoc. Alexei's condition was kept under wraps to protect him not only from scrutiny but also from injury.

The pressures placed upon the doomed family, especially Alexandra, affected them all, and they searched for support, which led to the appointment of the service of Grigory Yefimovich Rasputin. He had first been introduced to the family in 1903 as a healer at a tea he was invited to by the Montenegrin princesses Milica, and Anastasia. These princesses were also known by the term the "'Black Sisters'" and were very involved in mysticism. At the time, there were not many individuals from the upper echelon who were intrigued by, or even believed in, mysticism, and people, such as Rasputin, who were thought to have special powers. The sisters were already quite influential with their persuasions and recommendations over the royal family as they were understood to have sworn on their knees to help Alexandra conceive a son. They were determined to be taken in by the tsarina as their welcome to court was not an easy path due to their somewhat provincial backgrounds and their strange beliefs. The tsarina herself also struggled to be accepted and was lonely, so their friendship was inevitable, or written in the cards, so to speak.

Many hypnotists, physicians, and other healers were brought through the palace doors upon the instruction of the two sisters with no result in the arrival of a son and an heir to the throne until the arrival of a certain Dr. Philippe. A Frenchman, whose full name was Nizier Anthelme Philippe, was regarded as a mystic healer and miracle worker. He came from a poor background and had various successes in healing many people in France from the young age of 13. He became popular among the French elite as he continued practicing into his adult years, and his rooms were usually quite full of patients seeking his assistance. He had a checkered past and had been in trouble for practicing as a doctor without a license; however, he was acquitted on all the charges that were brought upon him. Milica had a successful outcome with him regarding the health of her own son and thought he would be ideal to help Alexandra's plight in trying to conceive a son. Alexandra harassed Nicholas into arranging the permission for him to come to Russia and practice as she thought he would be the answer they were looking for. After meeting him and being quite taken by his personality, Nicholas arranged for him to acquire a Doctor's Diploma from the Petersburg Military Medical Academy. Not only this prestige but also being awarded the rank of State Councilor, too! Nicholas's mother, Maria, his sister Xenia, and sister-in-law Ella were not convinced about Philippe and tried to dissuade the imperial couple against him when he was introduced to Alexandra and Nicholas by the sisters as someone who could potentially help them conceive a son. They would not hear of it and were completely taken by him and convinced that he would be able to help them.

In 1901 it seemed as though Alexandra was pregnant once again shortly after the birth of Anastasia, and Philippe assured her that it was a boy. He even suggested that if it was not a boy, he had the power to change it! He also convinced them not to seek any other doctor's advice or examination. Eventually after almost nine months had gone by and she should certainly have been physically showing her pregnancy, there seemed very little evidence she was pregnant. She finally submitted to an examination by the family doctor, Dr. Ott, who was present for the upcoming birth where it was discovered she was not pregnant at all. This condition is normally called a "phantom pregnancy," where the desire to be pregnant supersedes reality. The official announcement to the public was that she had a miscarriage that sadly did not earn her any sympathy. It just fueled even more imagined tales and ultimately yet another disappointment that the imperial couple could not produce a male heir. The stories about Philippe being more involved with the couple than just for healing got tongues wagging once again. The hypnosis practices he performed on the couple were said to have been done to influence political decisions and interference. Both Nicholas and Alexandra were loath to banish him, but eventually, this was the only choice they had. He left laden with gifts from them and departed with a prediction that she would meet someone soon who would speak to her of God. He also advised them to pray for the intervention of St. Seraphim, and this would finally grant them a son. The only St. Seraphim that could be found in Russia had been dead for more than 70 years! Nicholas ordered the exhumation of his remains and for them to bless him and to follow through the process to make him a saint. The tsar and tsarina both attended the ceremony and were completely captivated by the process, even immersing themselves in the Sarov River, which was known to be the bathing place of Seraphim. They were adamant in their belief that they would be blessed with a son.

Eventually, Alexandra fell pregnant once more and finally gave birth to a son on August 12, 1904, when Alexei Romanov was finally born. He was the first male heir to be born to a reigning tsar since the 17th century. It was a great time to celebrate for many but not for long. When it was discovered that Alexei suffered from hemophilia, it turned to panic. The sisters Milica and Anastasia were the first people Alexandra and Nicholas turned to for help. Their advice was to summon Grigory Rasputin. In 1905 when Rasputin was summoned by Nicholas and Alexandar to attend to a chronic bleeding occurrence of Alexei, they were desperate. Rasputin was successful in reducing the bleeding and was capable in alleviating the young child's misery, much to his parent's relief. He was quickly welcomed into the fold, and his words to the parents that he was now irrevocably linked to the destiny of both the child and them were taken seriously. He quickly became a trusted advisor and healer for the family. So how did he cure the child? There are accounts of Rasputin's advice to stop using aspirin, which had become a popular painkiller at that time. Rasputin was against any medication other than his own tinctures. We know now that aspirin is strongly advised not to be taken by hemophiliacs as it can prevent the clotting of blood. It could very well have been this simple omission of that medication that 'healed' Alexei.

Rasputin came from Siberia and was born into a poor family, and even though he did attend school, he was illiterate. When he reached his teenage years, he experienced a religious conversion and afterward declared himself to be not only a healer but also one who could predict the future. He ended up attending a monastery in Verkhoturye, and this is where he was greatly influenced by the secret Khlysty sect. This sect was an unorthodox group that had formed when they split from the Russian Orthodox Church and went underground to practice what they believed to be true. Among other things, they believed in repenting to its fullest form that could be by flagellation and even ritual orgies. Rasputin adapted his version of this belief system that to feel closest to God, one needed to feel "holy passionlessness," with him and that this was in his view a sensation ultimately reached through maintaining long sessions of sexual activity or debauchery. Rasputin ironically means "debauched one" in Russian. Becoming a monk was not in his destiny! He was not trusted by many and was well-known for his lewd and drunken behavior beyond the boundaries of the palace. This relationship he had with the tsar's family was just a feeding ground for growing contempt and distrust. Rasputin was conniving in his ways of influencing Alexandra, who he knew would, in turn, influence Nicholas. As it was a secret about Alexei's hemophilia, many could not understand and were quite deeply puzzled about what the attraction for Rasputin was.

His unkempt and scruffy appearance was unsettling for the members of the court, who were wary of this essentially strange and very odd man.

The certainty of the dangers the future tsar could be in, including the repercussions it could have on him, and deciding to keep his condition a secret ultimately led to the family withdrawing from society. The family was suffering such extreme repercussions from this retreat from society that they began to rely even more upon healers or mystics, such as Rasputin. He became the major influencer in their lives, particularly for Alexandra. Also, he began to gain even more power and influence over them. Alexandra completely believed that Rasputin had the power to cure this disease and even allowed Rasputin to hypnotize their child. It is possible to consider that he may even have hypnotized them, too!

Rasputin was almost worshiped by Alexandra, and even though he was not popular amongst their peers, this was brushed aside by her, blindly accepting him as a man far beyond what he really was. When he was in the confines of the palace, his demeanor was modest and holy-like; however, when he was outside these boundaries, his true colors shone. He had an insatiable sexual appetite and was known to brag and convince women that physical contact with him would enable healing for them. He was lewd and lubricious, and even when reports of his unsavory behavior were sent to Nicholas, they were met with refusal and disbelief. Often those that dared to try to convince the monarchy of his alter ego behavior beyond the walls of the palace were relocated to remote locations of service or were relieved of their positions.

In 1911, Rasputin's conduct became so out of control that eventually the tsar decided to banish him. There were many rumors surfacing of sexual involvement with the tsarina, but none of this was ever proven although it has been said that there were some notes that have surfaced with passionate letters from Alexandra to Rasputin. His banishment only lasted a mere few months until Alexandra reinstated him once again. Rasputin's power over her was great. Thereafter, he was firmly entrenched, and Nicholas did not want to upset his wife nor put his son at risk as Rasputin had managed to relieve his suffering. Rasputin was instrumental in assisting Alexandra with her suffering in dealing with the stress of having a hemophilic child and her own health issues. She developed a deep trust for him and his powers.

Nicholas was devoted to his family and was easily swayed by his wife's stronger character and ideals. When Nicholas was away at war in 1915, Alexandra was placed as consort in charge of dealing with Russian affairs in his absence. Rasputin, who was already her close confidant, became her adviser in governmental affairs. Alexandra was fickle in her behavior of dismissing ministers that Rasputin recommended to her to remove from their positions and replacing them with others that were not fit for the position, thus causing a collapse of the administration. Huge distrust was growing rapidly of Alexandra's rule, and she was even thought to be a secret agent for the Germans at one time! There were many instances where efforts were made to try to murder Rasputin by those that saw through his tricks, but he was protected by Alexandra.

Nicholas the Troubled Tsar

With such little guidance, Nicholas stumbled his way into his reign causing many upsets along the way. He was greatly influenced by his wife who advised him on seeking the confidence of spiritual healers and faith practitioners. His advisors were unscrupulous men who were after securing their own wealth and stability and poorly advised him, giving him a contorted view of what was actually going on in reality. Nicholas almost seemed to rule with a blissful unawareness. It was said that his journal, where he was meant to be logging official government policies, was filled with entries of the day-to-day occurrences that were happening with his wife and children. He was a devoted family man, but it was evident that he either totally forgot, or just did not care too much, about his governmental responsibilities.

He did not have complete faith in his advisers as he also felt they were somewhat beneath his intellectual level, and as an autocrat and a sovereign, he was chosen by God so his power was absolute. It was rather delusional as he didn't even want this huge responsibility of power but pretended he did. He was dedicated to the autocratic way of life and had unyielding views about self-governance and a form of independence. Any uprisings or negative actions against him were met with the full force of the police upon the instigators. He regarded those who were against him or disagreed with his ideas to be conspiring against him.

When it came to foreign policy he simply had no idea what was going on and made endless blunders, such as going through the procedures of aligning with Germany's Emperor William II when Russia was already in an alliance with them. This kind of inferior knowledge that he should have been aware of and was not was embarrassing for his counterparts. He was forced to establish an elected legislature much to his displeasure as it defied his beliefs of autocracy and royal rule. The rise of industrialization and urbanization in Russia was growing at a rapid pace and placed huge demands on the government, with issues of loyalty from both the intellectuals and the impoverished increasing. Nicholas was not one for public participation in affairs of the government, and during his first political address, he made this clear. Representatives from local councils were rebuked by him as having no place in making decisions and that these important structures and processes lay firmly in the hands of the hierarchy. He had a misguided and confused way of thinking leadership should be affected, almost as if he was the "father of the people" who needed to be led and reprimanded with a firm hand when they stepped out of line. This did not fare well for his popularity among a huge part of the population.

During the 1890s Russia's exponential expansion into the Far East was evident with the construction of the Trans-Siberian railroad network. This connected Russia with the Pacific, and this was seen as a threat by the Japanese. His determination to have the progress of Russia's foothold in the East was admirable, but it also led to war in 1904 with Japan that ended with the Treaty of Portsmouth being signed in 1905.

Chapter 5:

Russo-Japanese War and

Bloody Sunday

Nicholas found himself in the midst of a massive problem that had been brewing since Russia's defeat in the Crimean War between 1853 and 1856. Keeping the Romanov empire and its rule strong was a challenge with the need for modernization, education, and development. It was a conundrum to be faced that threatened the usual way of how the empire was run. The constant demands placed on the government with urbanization rapidly growing and the support needed for both educational and economic reform was starting to show some serious cracks in the strength the Romanovs always had achieved as leaders.

The massive divide between the elite and the poor widened with the latter becoming more and more fed up with their leader. Nicholas was committed to the industrial growth of Russia, but he did not welcome public participation, choosing to stick to the hierarchical method instead. Russia was the largest country in the world in the late 1800s and ruled by what was known as the "pillars of autocracy," which were the army, civil service, and the Russian Orthodox Church.

Right up until 1905 there was no elected parliament; there was only the power of the tsar. He was the ultimate rule of authority over all issues of governing the country with no scope for any change to it either. It was as if the writing was on the wall for drastic change as the world became more modern and developed.

When Nicholas came into power quite suddenly, he was ill-prepared, and the tsar rule that had existed for the past 300 years began to crumble. The civil service that relied on positions of power through loyalty to the monarchy securing their roles were poorly paid, leading to brewing discontent. They were an easy target to be bribed as their service to the tsar was not recognized through how good they were at their jobs but how long they had served.

The Okhrana was formed as a secret police for the tsar that had almost unlimited powers on what they could do to the citizens. This included arrests, intimidation, spying, torture, murder, and the ability to exile anyone who was against the tsar to the far reaches of Siberia. The idea was to get them so far away into isolation that they posed no threat to the tsar.

The Russian army consisted of only nobility in the senior roles. They were well paid and flourished. The peasants only had the positions of soldiers, with no hope of promotion, and they were poorly paid and made to live in extremely harsh conditions. The training of these soldiers was also neglected to leave most of the "army work" to be carried out by the Cossacks, who were the mounted cavalry unit and the greatest supporters of the tsar.

A tsar was to be the head of the Russian Orthodox Church, appointed by God and was not to be considered otherwise.

Part of the strength of the tsar would be determined by their level of utmost faith in the church. When it came to the peasants' belief in God, they were greatly influenced by the church and the messages of faith that were preached. They were taught to accept their status in life. To consider their life differently was not even an option. Considering that most of the population was illiterate and many had no form or hope of being educated, the power was in the priests' hands to guide them to their fate. By the time Nicholas came into power, this had all started to change.

There were different class systems in Russia. The ruling class was the tsar and his family followed by the nobility, who were dependent on the tsar and had a mutually beneficial relationship. The middle class was the educated people, such as businessmen, lawyers, doctors, and the like. This class, in particular, was more open to change as it had exposure and experience to how other countries were run. Then came the working class, who were the backbone of the country, keeping the cogs turning but poorly paid and also living in terrible conditions considering the amount of work they had to do. Finally, there were the peasants that made up most of the population and were mostly owned by landowners. It was only in 1861 when serfdom was abolished by Alexander II that there was meant to be a significant change for this class. Unfortunately, they ended up even worse off by the corrupt landowners who tried to profit off them! The irony of it all was that even though Russia was heading for more industrialization, landowners had no need to invest in machines to do the work that a poorly paid serf could do for them. Once serfdom was abolished, the landowners could now convert the earnings they had to pay the peasants into rentals now, as the peasants had to live somewhere. It was truly a terrible time for peasants.

There was a stumbling block, too, when it came to implementing industry as the infrastructure was not in place yet to support it. Roads, railways, and the skills required to work machines were just not prevalent. The main issue with the failure of industrialization was that it was not led by the government as it was in other countries but by the middle classes that had more to lose than to gain in their eyes. They could not see the worth of it when they had a workforce in place already.

The growing discontentment of the masses was a sure grounding for unrest, protests, and strikes. The poorly thought out process of freeing these peasants from serfdom was a disaster. The peasants would need land to live on after being set free, but then, of course, this land would need to be paid for by the landowners (the original owners of these people). What was formed was a payment system called Redemption Payments, where the peasants would pay back the 'loan' of the land they lived on. This placed even more pressure on already oppressed people. They were farmers mostly and were the part of the population that was expected to not only provide their food but also to provide even more for export. It was a dire situation.

In addition to the state of the rural part of Russia, the towns were suffering, as well. The expanding urbanization was also poorly planned, and suddenly the towns were bursting at the seams. There was not enough housing for all the workers, and people were living in appalling and unhealthy situations. Disease and sickness spread easily, and the number of deaths was high. The conditions people had to work in were shocking, and the hours were extraordinarily long (11.5-hour days)! There was no such thing as workers' unions to protect their rights as these were banned outright. There were also not near enough jobs for all the people who flocked to the towns seeking work.

In short, Russia was in terrible turmoil, and the ineptitude of the tsar was clear to many.

The Russo-Japanese War

Mounting military forces of strength, both to the east with Japan and to the west of Russia with Germany, were becoming problematic. The Russo-Japanese War broke out in 1904 with the Japanese attack on a Russian fleet of ships in Port Arthur. Russia and Japan had many disagreements in the lead up to this event about the command of Manchuria. Japan was feeling undermined by Russia's antics with the occupation of Port Arthur. In 1894, there was the 'Triple Intervention," where Russia, France, and Germany teamed up to resolve the issue, which resulted in Japan relinquishing its claim on the ports in South Manchuria and the Liaodong Peninsula.

When Japan tried to retaliate, it caused obvious clashes between the two countries. The establishment of the Trans-Siberian Railway by the Russians that went through Manchuria was the final straw for the Japanese. The Japanese tried more than once to find a way to settle this conflict by sending diplomats to Russia to reach a compromise. Even though an agreement was met between the nations, Russia did not uphold its agreement to withdraw troops from Manchuria. Unable to reach any agreements and being treated with disrespect by not even being permitted an audience with the tsar himself, they ran out of patience.

The attack in Port Arthur took the Russians by surprise as they never thought Japan would wage war against them, and it resulted in an eventual victory for Japan. Once Japan had bombarded the Russian naval fleet in Port Arthur with great success, it continued with strength in its attack on land, cutting off Russia's army that was en route to support the navy. Japan was well organized, far better than Russia, and continued to gain success in their siege against them. As the fight for power over this significant port intensified over the next year, there were many losses on both sides. Russia's fleet was destroyed in the Battle of Tsushima, ending with Japan not only winning on water but on land, too. Russia, one of the largest countries in the world, suffered embarrassing defeats against an Asian country countless times. One of Russia's commanders just gave up their command post without consultation with the officers, even though they still had the firepower and sufficient supplies to continue their assault against Japanese soldiers. It was as if they just surrendered. Great numbers as high as 60,000 Russian and 41,000 Japanese soldiers were lost, and apart from human loss, the economic loss was monumental for both countries.

The Treaty of Portsmouth

The Russian people were mortified at the lack of prowess their tsar had and his utter lack of skill and diplomacy to lead once more. Finally, after the successful Battle of Tsushima, Japan asked the United States President Theodore Roosevelt to intervene and assist in negotiating a peace treaty. This suited Roosevelt well as an ongoing war between Russia and Japan would not help his plans to defeat China.

Negotiations were very difficult with a stalemate of both sides wanting control of Sakhalin Island, and Russia wanting to keep their fleet in the Pacific. Apart from this, Russia vehemently declined to pay any war cost compensation to Japan. Eventually, Japan agreed to half of the southern part of the island with no monetary compensation as it was clear that Russia had no way, nor any intention, of paying it in any event.

The Treaty of Portsmouth was signed on August 9, 1905 in Maine in the United States, which ultimately ended the Russo-Japanese War. It was agreed that Japan would control Korea and most of South Manchuria, which included Port Arthur. The railway that crossed this area would also be under their control. Russia was forced into this compromise as it did not have the financial means and had, in reality, lost the war. In the interests of peace, this agreement was finally reached after much mediation by Roosevelt. He received a Nobel Peace Prize for his work in reaching this peace agreement between the two countries.

The people of Japan were unhappy with the long-awaited outcome of the agreement as they felt they had won the war but had still lost so much as Russia did not have to pay any war costs. Similarly, the Russian people were also disappointed in having to give up half of Sakhalin to Japan and having to acknowledge that Japan was the dominant power in Korea.

The citizens of the United States sided with Japan as, in their eyes, this affront Japan had taken upon Russia was justified. This momentous event in the history of the United States and Japan's cooperation was short-lived as rivalry continued to grow between these two nations. Strangely enough, the association between Russia and Japan after the treaty was signed, and despite all the fighting and loss, began to mend.

This event in history was a pivotal moment with Russia finding itself in a precarious position with all the unrest growing on their home ground, which was one of the factors that led to the eventuality of the Russian Revolution in 1905.

Bloody Sunday

Things came to a head in Russia with the working class reaching a critical point and countless strikes being held in St. Petersburg. Workers were bitterly disappointed with what they thought would be a better future for them and their families by moving to the cities to work. The desperate living conditions were only getting worse, and the people were hungry, angry, and scared for their futures.

There were many reasons for this march upon the palace, including that peasants were poorly compensated for their work and they were not permitted to sell, nor mortgage, the land that they owned. Extreme suffering due to low income and housing that was seriously inadequate with no plumbing or running water caused diseases to be spread quickly and created an unhealthy environment. The average working day was 11 hours and 10 hours on a Saturday, leaving little time for workers to rest or spend time with their families. There was little or no concern for the health and safety of the workforce. Trade unions were strictly banned, and workers had no voice, no representation to instill any change upon their conditions.

What was meant to be a peaceful demonstration on January 22, 1905, with tens of thousands of workers gathered to march to the Winter Palace in St. Petersburg to try to improve their working conditions, ended up being a total massacre.

Georgy Gapan, a radicalized priest who was a stalwart in his support of the welfare of the poor, had arranged this march and forbade the attendees from bringing any weapons. Only religious icons and pictures of the Russian royal family were permitted. A petition that outlined all their grievances was brought with the peaceful protesters to present to the tsar. The event was planned for the people to present their issues to the tsar and ask for his help.

The petition that was signed by over 150,000 people, was long but was simply worded and contained not only the grievances of the workers and inhabitants of St. Petersburg, but it was also a plea from their families, too. They wanted justice and security from their sovereign. The oppression and burdens upon them were too much, and even though serfdom was to have been abolished, they still felt as if they were bound by the same restrictions but worse off. The tsar himself believed he was chosen by God, and many of the devoutly religious peasants asked in the petition if this treatment they have had to endure was within the law of God. A break of church and state ruling together was included in the petition.

With the lack of rights and respect for the work that they did, life was becoming more difficult and intolerable. The decision to leave their work for this day to march upon the palace and demand their rights was long overdue as any action they had tried to pursue with their employers was not heard. The employers refused to hear them stating that they had no right to object to their conditions and should do as they were instructed. Slavery still existed clearly but just in a different form.

The hours that these workers were meant to work were beyond comprehension, and the demand was to reduce these to a more attainable eight hours a day. There were many issues when it came to wages and the rates they were paid, with no consultation or representation. The need for a union was desperate but was not allowed. Any move to air their plight to their employers was met with abuse, intolerance, and even exile. They also wanted those that were exiled to be freed and allowed to come back to work but in better conditions.

When it came to collecting redemption payments from the workers to "pay for their land," they had no say in how it was spent, nor knew what was done with it. The people wanted to have a better system in place when it came to the collection of taxes and government expenditures. Freedom of speech, media, gatherings, and religion also featured, and education for all paid for by the government was among some of the important changes that they wanted to institute.

This petition was a desperate cry for help to be part of making Russia a great country with the tsar as their leader. It was to even the scales with representation from all classes and to place some control over the bureaucrats who were benefiting from this situation they were in. It was not to overthrow the tsar, nor storm the palace.

Nicholas was not there to receive the petition as he had been advised to not be present (again badly advised, and one can only ponder the outcome of this event if he had been there to receive the petition). The army that awaited this massive crowd of people was commanded to fire into the crowd on the assumption and instruction that this crowd of protestors was intending to hurt the tsar and sabotage the palace. Even though the tsar had not personally ordered the firing into the crowd, he was ultimately responsible for the deaths of hundreds of his people. This day in history is called Bloody Sunday and was clearly the provocation of the beginning of the Russian Revolution of 1905.

Russia erupted following Bloody Sunday with a series of strikes and unrest across the country that brought more chaos and disruption. For reasons apart from the devastating loss of life and the violent outcome of Bloody Sunday, people were angry at the defeat of Russia by the Japanese, tired of suffering economic hardship, and had little faith in the leadership of Nicholas. Political opposition and influential revolutionaries were making a lot more sense to the general public of Russia. Russian troops were sent to bring order to the unrest that often had violent outcomes. The Revolution of 1905 erupted.

The Russian Revolution of 1905

Even though the Revolution of 1905 was short—just over two years—it was powerful enough to show how discontent the people of Russia were and that change was imminent. The wave that was sparked by Bloody Sunday spread rapidly across the country with strikes and unrest. Apart from all the unrest in Russia, this movement spread across to the Baltic provinces of Georgia, Poland, and Finland, with the uprising of nationalist movements to represent the oppressed. Russia's downtrodden people and the stance they took had started a massive movement. The Russian Prime Minister Sergei Witte's efforts at governance served little result. Anger was brewing, stirred by the loss of the Russo-Japanese War and the subsequent Bloody Sunday atrocity. All the reasons that the petition stated were not being seriously taken and more discontent kept rising. The multiethnicity of Russia created a plethora of problems since the late 1800s and the attempt of Russification policies being enforced made it even worse. Polish people were seen as a threat to the tsar, and their culture was severely squashed by the government, creating much resentment. These growing issues only added fuel to the fire even more in the revolution with people demanding their rights.

Agricultural challenges were plentiful with prices falling rapidly for grain from Russia, resulting in the deterioration of farming activities. The demand for imports grew, and the continued push of industrialization through heavy taxing of peasants was unsustainable. Those who worked on the Russian railways and in similar types of manual labor intensive jobs were the lowest-paid individuals in Europe, and even though the cost of living may have been less than in other countries, the workers could still not afford a basic quality of life, stirring up more rebellion and anger among the masses.

A general strike in Russia that began on October 7, 1905 with a railroad strike and spread rapidly into many of the big cities was the pinnacle that made the tsar react and think of what was to be done to quell the violence and uprising. Other strikes before this one did not satisfy the strikers' demands, so this massive strike was inevitable. The power the strikers had by mobilizing the railroad industry affected all industries massively. The collaborative efforts among workers to demand change were quite remarkable. It did not matter if they were from small shops or large factories to banking and educational institutions, to people who drove the trams. Students began to riot at the injustice of the political and educational system. It was evident that it was not only the oppressed and poor people that had issues. Unrest was spreading to the educated and upper social classes, too. Notably, discontent among the upper classes had already begun back in 1904, when groups of liberals found a loophole in the law against political gatherings and began to host a succession of banquets. Discussions were held about necessary political reforms and the need for a constitution.

This movement across Russia ultimately shut down St. Petersburg, which was hugely beneficial concerning their demands. Trade unions were formed, and the representation that workers were seeking was finally coming to fruition. The land was seized by peasants, and the unmet expectations for change created even more unrest and were dealt with by force by the obstinate government refusing to submit to their demands. It seemed that there was no end in sight.

Nicholas eventually responded on October 30, 1905 to attempt to quell the unrest with what is famously known as the October Manifesto and the establishment of the Duma. When the October Manifesto and the Duma were created, they promised to present both political change and freedom for the citizens of Russia. This quelled the revolution but did not completely satisfy the working force, as there was little change to their circumstances and much unhappiness.

Despite the massive movement of the Revolution of 1905 that was hugely significant in history, only a few of the demands were met and those that weren't continued to be fought for going forward. Uprisings and demands by those that have been oppressed is still evident in today's society. The reshaping of life in Russia was the expectation of many, and the disappointment in the autocracy that continued to not take this seriously was deeply harmful to the tsar's rule. Despite the uprising not resulting in the shift of power from the tsar, it did make way for a wide range of changes in that time.

The October Manifesto and the Role of the Duma

The powers of the promised elected legislature, the Duma, were quite limited even though it was formed to be a constitutional monarchy to alleviate the plight of the oppressed workforce and give them a voice. The budget was severely constrained, and international policies did not form part of the portfolio. Most importantly, the October Manifesto allowed the tsar to continue to retain the right to veto any decision or suggestions presented. It was a bit of a farce, still leaving power firmly in the hands of the autocracy. The motivating factor of this manifesto was, after all, to mark the end of autocracy, which it didn't. The forming of the Duma did little to placate the Russian workforce as it was yet another oversight by Nicholas in not dealing with the issue at hand and refusing to find a compromise and a more representative style of governing. What was awoken was the growing support for mainly the Bolsheviks and other revolutionary groups throughout the country. The Bolsheviks, or also known as the Reds or Red Army formed in 1917 as a result of a divide in the Russian Social-Democratic Workers' Party. Bolshevik translated into English means "one of the majority." It was led by Vladimir Lenin, and they would eventually become the Communist Party of the Soviet Union. There was also a great divide with the liberals leaning towards choosing to function within the new system as they were wary of another revolution and the consequences of it and the Marxists, who represented the communists, and the Populists, who represented the common people, being vehemently against it.

The Union of the Liberation was the first liberal group that was formed in Russia under the leadership of Peter Berngardovich, a prior Marxist. Beginning in January 1904 it was founded in St. Petersburg and had to operate undercover to achieve its objectives among which were to replace the dictatorship with a democratic monarchy. In time the name was changed to the Constitutional Democrats. Most of the votes in the first Duma election were won by them. Nicholas was reeling from the change that he knew was the beginning of the end of autocracy, and he struggled to find ways to make it work for him to continue to have control. The Duma was more of a consultative organization with no power and included representation from landowners and business people, the middle class, and both academics and peasants. The number of representatives in total was around 500 and fluctuated over the years of its existence. This very first Duma was terminated by Nicholas and was known as "the Duma of people's anger." There have been several Dumas formed over the years, and currently, one still exists in modern Russia.

Changes that the revolution accomplished began with the formation of the October Manifesto, and this is where the establishment of Duma was created. The manifesto was so heavily encompassed with issues that were difficult to resolve, and no clear path of how to resolve them. A constitution was still needed, and only in 1906 was one presented that gave the monarchy limited powers with its new government structure. The Romanov dynasty held on by its fingertips until the outbreak of World War I when even more devastating events lay in wait.

Chapter 6:

The Fall of Rasputin, Onset

of the Great War, and

Revolution

Grigory Rasputin died on December 30, 1916, after a year that was more than likely his most powerful one. During this time, he was serving as the personal advisor of Empress Alexandra, and he affected many changes within the government with his strong influence over her and the decisions she made. He inappropriately ruled the country through his persuasion. Many rumors trickled through the palace about Rasputin, even as far as him having a supposed affair with the Empress. These rumors were not only about her but also many other aristocratic women. He was perceived by most to be a disgrace and was not welcome in court. He was lewd, and he had a reputation of many sexual encounters with women from all the classes that he tricked into thinking he was a healer with special powers. He obviously had charisma and a way with women, and he continued to be sought after. He had gained knowledge of tinctures and herbs so did provide a positive outcome for some ailments, especially in the case of Alexei's condition.

There were many attempts on his life from powerful noblemen including Prince Felix Yusupov, Vladimir Mitrofanovich Purishkevich, and Grand Duke Dmitry Pavlovich, who were instrumental in creating a great conspiracy to prevent further scandal for the monarchy that was caused by Rasputin and to finally get rid of him. It was only in 1916 that their plot to murder him was successful.

Some stories about his death have become legendary folklore tales. Among them was that fatal day for Rasputin in December when he was fed tea cakes that were laced with poison (likely cyanide) after he was tricked into going to Yusupov's home. Yusupov was not only one of the richest men in Russia at the time, but he was also the husband of the tsar's niece Irina. Yusupov was not viewed as a powerful or admirable man by the royal family, and one of the reasons was his refusal to enlist in the army. This plot of vengeance against Rasputin allowed Yusupov to become someone to be admired for this cunning plan and the ultimate removal of Rasputin from the royal household. Apart from this reason, it was also a chance for the family to influence Nicholas rather than Alexandra and Rasputin. The stature of the monarchy and the need to remove the overwhelming power that Rasputin had were vitally important to this group of conspirators.

Although Rasputin was warned against going by some of his friends that night, he decided to go anyway. The myth says that he did not die from the poison that would have certainly killed someone and that Yusupov apparently panicked because it was not working and taking so long to have any influence so he ended up shooting Rasputin. However, this also did not result in his death! It was said that after being shot by Yusopov, Rasputin managed to get himself up and run outside to where Purishkevich apparently shot him again. He was viciously beaten and then bound with rope. His body was tossed into the mostly ice-covered waters of the Neva River. In later years, an autopsy that was performed on his remains revealed water in his lungs that strongly suggests he was alive when he was underwater. Another story was that an autopsy revealed his cause of death was by gunshot at close range to the head.

Other rumors about Rasputin were that he was engaged with the Germans as an undercover spy trading secrets. There were other whimsical murmurings of him planning to begin an epidemic with apples that had been poisoned with cholera.

Alexandra was distraught upon hearing the news of his death, and it made her even more determined to continue leading Russia by autocratic rule. Little did she know that the revolution was imminent. Eerily, Rasputin had written to Nicholas shortly before his death that he had a premonition that he was going to die soon, and if it was by the hands of government officials, the entire family would suffer the same fate. This prophecy he had was to prove true a mere 15 months later.

Much to the shock of the conspirators of Rasputin's murder, the change they expected did not happen. The Bolsheviks spun the story around in their favor, showing the nobles as being corrupt. They said the murder of Rasputin was only a sign of the nobles' persistent need for ultimate control over all of Russia. Rasputin ended up being a scapegoat for Russia's problems. The joining of forces between the moderates and the Bolsheviks following these events created a massive opposition that called for the tsar's abdication.

Aleksandr Dmitriyevich Protopopov, who was the minister of the interior, did his utmost to become the Empress's confidant and advisor by attempting to convince her that Rasputin's spirit had entered him and that he now had his powers. He had little persuasion over her despite his ramblings and moments of apparent visions. In a matter of months after Rasputin's death, riots erupted in the streets. The streets were lined with red flags and complete chaos ensued. Protopopov retaliated with the full force of machine gunfire being shot into the marauding mobs only to be met with even more violence and death to any person who was in the army or the police by the hands of the mobs. His measures generated little change and just made the situation take a turn for the worse.

The Onset of the Great War

The onset of World War I saw multiple empires crushed—Turkey, Germany, Austria-Hungary, and of course, Russia. The exact moment or reason why World War I broke out is disputed by many, but it is mostly believed that this war was ultimately sparked by the assassination of Archduke Franz Ferdinand of Austria in 1914 by Serbian nationalists. It launched a war across Europe that continued until 1918. The consequences of this war brought horrific scenes of trench warfare, poisonous gas, and great tanks, resulting in many deaths on all sides of the battlefields. The Great War was also thought to have been a final straw in events leading up to it that had been simmering across many countries since the late 1800s.

When Russia decided to enter the war, the differences in opinions and strategies of how to fight only led to even more resentment at Nicholas's rule. Serbia appealed to Russia to help them, and it took less than a week for Russia, France, Great Britain, and Belgium to join forces against Germany and Austria-Hungary. As Russia entered into the war in 1914, Nicholas did his best to lead his countrymen to victory, but this failed. Gaping divides among the leadership of their priorities when planning attacks was hugely evident when researching war chronicles and most of these disputes were among the higher echelon of leadership. Additionally, his throne was in turmoil under the leadership of his influenced wife and just exacerbated his problems.

Russia was not prepared for war when that fateful decision on July 24, 1914 was taken to enter into it. Germany had been dominant in its influence over Russia since the Russo-Japanese War, and the monarchy had had enough of being undermined. Even though this move to enter the war would antagonize the Germans, the ministers were determined to take a stand of strength to defend Russia and to collaborate with other countries that were against German and Austrian forces. The Russian army was still reeling from the aftermath of the war ten years prior, but this was discarded as a reason, and honor and survival were the deciding factors.

Russia had an enormous death toll resulting from the war, with over 1.8 million in the military and around 1.5 million civilians perishing. In 1915, Nicholas decided to retain the personal command of his army. Although this might have been a brave decision, it was a very poor one due to his incompetence as an accomplished leader. The unrelenting force of the Germans proved too much for the Russians. The ongoing dispute between the war minister, Vladimir Sukhomlinov, and Nicholas created hostility and affected leadership greatly. During the spring of 1915, Russian forces had to retreat, which caused serious numbers of refugees to seek solace in Russian cities that were unable to provide it.

The hardships that Russia faced with limited food and a crumbling economy fueled not only the disgruntled forces but also the peasants and the poor who were starving. Growing hostility for Nicholas also stemmed from the reason that his wife was of German descent and was ruling their country while their tsar was waging his futile attempts in the battle of the war, which just added more fuel to the proverbial fire. Nicholas's slim grip of order over his country was in serious trouble. No men were at home to farm, so they relied on imports that were not forthcoming due to the war blocking passage. Transportation systems collapsed, and the economy was stifled, creating a destitute state. When Russia entered the war, it was strong in its capacity of transportation structure, but this had dwindled to less than half of what it was originally. Nicholas had enforced a ban on alcohol in a misguided attempt to boost morale and instill more productivity, but all this did was deplete the treasury of tax revenue and resulted in the further demise of Russia's financial status. Russia was ready to explode once more, which would lead to the end of its participation in World War I and the end of tsar rule.

The Russian Revolution of 1917

There were multiple pleas received from both the tsar's brother the Grand Duke Michael Alexandrovich and also the current president of the Duma Mikhail Rodzianko upon Nicholas to take action. They plead with him to place measures to counteract the violence that was mounting and the immediate need for a new government. Prince Golitsyn, who was the president of the council of ministers, also pleaded with him but nothing could change Nicholas's plan of action. He dismissed the Grand Duke's advice and continued with his plan to send more troops into St. Petersburg that was now known as Petrograd. (The name changed in 1914 due to the negative feelings against Germany and the name sounding "too German." It later changed back to St. Petersburg in 1924). When Nicholas sent his troops into Petrograd in an attempt to combat the violent uprising of the revolution, he was blindly unaware of where his actions would ultimately lead. He was informed poorly by Minister of the Interior Alexander Propotov that the situation was under control. The soldiers, who were initially sent out on February 26 to sort out the unrest where 200,000 people were gathered and protesting, ended up joining the demonstrators against the police. These soldiers were young and easily influenced plus lacked any formal training. On the morning of March 11, it all ended in disarray, and despite Nicholas's attempts to send reinforcements and dissolve the Duma, the control of the city was lost, and chaos spread. By March 12, regiments had rebelled and joined together, wreaking havoc and raiding the arsenal stores. Government buildings were set alight, including the Ministry of the Interior, the courts, and the police head office among others. It was total carnage, and more than 60,000 soldiers had joined the protestors and taken control of the city, resulting in what became the beginning of the Revolution of 1917.

All this turmoil reached a crescendo while World War I was in progress. It did not make a good foundation for the home front while the country was at war. Many Russians initially were supportive of the war to retain respect and hopefully gain some power, but it dismally failed for the most part. Nicholas's frequent dissolving of the Duma on a whim did little to appease the Russian public as it seemed he would do this each time the Duma went against him.

In desperation for order, on February 27 the Duma created a Provisional Committee that later became the Provisional Government. This period is known as the February Revolution. The first order of business was to issue a demand of abdication upon Nicholas. It was not only the general public of Russia that were losing faith in the leadership capabilities of the tsar, but pressure was also coming from six of the seven commanders at the time, who were calling for his abdication. There was little faith in Nicholas, and the plan was that his brother Mikhail Alexandrovich, who was the Grand Duke of Russia, would become tsar. The duke refused. However, instead of quelling the Revolution of 1917, it fired it up dramatically. The idea was that the abdication would ignite more substantial support for the war effort. They were ill-prepared by the refusal of Nicholas's brother to assume the position of the tsar.

As a consequence of the revolution, the Petrograd Soviet was formed, which was made up of soldiers and striking workers along with the new Provisional Government. They were of the view that the efforts of the revolution would highlight the urgent necessity to address the food crisis and other challenges that had arisen from the war under the poor leadership of Nicholas. They did not fully understand the enormous challenges that lay ahead for them.

Lenin and the Bolsheviks

The leader of the Bolshevik revolutionary party, Vladimir Lenin, left Switzerland at the start of the uprising with the objective to assume control of the revolution. Embittered by the death of his elder brother at the hands of the Romanov empire, Lenin had only contempt for the tsar and what his family represented. Lenin was a very astute man who had one goal—to rid Russia of tsarist rule.

When his brother was executed for his involvement in the assassination of Alexander III, Lenin was drawn to the cause of the revolutionaries. He circulated among Marxist groups while studying law. When he qualified, he established his law practice in St. Petersburg and was deeply involved in the Union for the Struggle for the Liberation of the Working Class. Their drive was to increase the number of supporters of Marxist values. In 1895, Lenin was arrested with other leaders of the Union and was imprisoned for a year, followed by exile to Siberia for a further three.

When his exile was completed in 1900, he traveled to Western Europe, where he officially became known as Lenin. He was born Vladimir Ilyich Ulyanov in 1870. The time he spent in Western Europe was focused on bringing socialism to Russia. There were challenges along the way with a parting of the Russian Social-Democratic Workers'

Party (RSDWP) with the Bolsheviks, and the Mensheviks having alternate views on the socialism movement. In 1912, Lenin officially formed the Bolshevik Party. When the Russian Revolution of 1905 broke out, Lenin traveled back to Russia hoping to be part of the changes. Nicholas's forming a constitution and an elected government helped to restore order although he reneged on these. In any event, that ultimately forced Lenin back into exile. Lenin was not a supporter of World War I and worked to create a growing rebellion among the soldiers.

At the peak of the February Revolution, Germany allowed Lenin passage through their territory from Switzerland in the hopes that Lenin would quell the Russian effort in the war with his influence. It only took eight months for the monarchy to collapse and for the Bolsheviks to take over. In 1917, the Bolsheviks led by Lenin brought the end of Russia's participation in World War I with an armistice reached. The withdrawal from the war was motivated by the desperate need to feed the Russian population. Britain and France were approached by Leon Trotsky, who was head of foreign affairs, to motivate peace talks, but this failed. Russia then went ahead to pursue its own appeal of peace to Germany and Austria that was acknowledged, thus forming the Brest-Litovsk agreement. Months of discussions followed, and eventually an agreement was reached. However, Russia not only lost a massive part of its territory in the deal that was concluded but also one-third of its population, too. Coal, oil, and iron stores were among these critical areas as well that would cause unrest in the future.

Lenin called this an acceptance of "shameful peace" to prevent a world revolution. The war had destroyed Russia's economy, and the options were limited.

What Did the Revolution of 1917 Mean for Russia in the Future?

Russia has mostly been considered separate from Europe, particularly after the Revolution of 1917. The formation of a democratic government in the form of the Provisional Government led by Alexander Kerensky was welcomed but was not instrumental in the long term.

The arrival of Lenin and the Bolsheviks post-revolution caused much trepidation among the Russian public. Their withdrawal from the war and peace with Germany essentially cut Russia off from Europe. The war was, in the view of Lenin and his compatriots, purely for monarchical gain and was far afield from his communist culture. His view was that the war should be put aside, and forgotten, not even to commemorate any victories they may have had.

The Russian Society of Soldiers Who Fell in the War had memorial statues or monuments built in their honor as a remembrance of what they had sacrificed. It was only two years later in 1918 that Lenin decreed these statues be removed and replaced with new symbols of people who had been effective in the revolutionary sector instead. His view was that these statues represented "slaves of service to the tsar" and did not represent the Russia he envisioned.

When Lenin became the world's first leader of a Marxist state, one of the notable things he did was to create the

Cheka, which was the first secret police force in Russia. He used this organization to not only control the opposition but also to muzzle anyone who challenged him. In a drastic response to an assassination attempt, he retaliated with a force called the Red Terror. Mass executions were held of anyone opposing the Communist Party, or thought to be supporters of the tsar regime. It is thought around 100,000 people were executed during this time of the Red Terror.

From 1917 until 1927 there was a dramatic transformation of Russia into a socialist state that was known as the Soviet Union. This is broken into two periods—Soviet Russia from 1917 up to 1922 and Soviet Union, or the Union of Soviet Socialist Republics (USSR), from 1922 to 1991.

The Soviet Union remained in place until 1991 and up until then any form of symbolism to these soldiers was only found outside of Russia. East Prussia, Warsaw, Prague, Belgrade, and even Berlin represent the sacrifices made by these soldiers in the name of their tsar. In Soissons and Verdun in France, some areas of the cemeteries there were allocated for Russian soldiers. In Seattle, Washington a monument was eventually erected in 1936 to commemorate 1,700,000 Russian soldiers who served under the tsar after much discussion among the Soviet Veterans Society and the Russian Orthodox Church.

Interestingly during the 1930s, the Red Army, which was one of the stalwarts of the Soviet Union, reviewed this time of war between Germany and Russia in great detail, taking all the strategies and events during the conflict to establish much of the indoctrination of the armed services.

Once the Soviet Union was at the end of its quest to be a communist society views began to change. In the Moscow

City Cemetery, crosses were placed by tsarism supporters in 2004 and called the "Memorial Park Complex for the Heroes of World War One." Great changes to the government were evident in 2010 resulting in a law being passed by President Vladimir Putin in 2012 to associate August 1 with the day Russia entered into the war and also decree it to be a special military holiday. In 2014, a monument was erected to commemorate those that had been perhaps forgotten during the time of Nicholas II's rule.

Chapter 7:

The Abdication and Arrest of

Nicholas II and His Family

The abdication of Nicholas II is what many associate as being the most prevalent point in Russia's history. He not only abdicated for himself but also for his son on March 15, 1917. He appointed his brother Grand Duke Michael Alexandrovich to succeed him, thinking that this would keep power under tsar rule, but Michael refused the very next day. He would not accept the title unless it was by agreement of the democratic action, which it was not. He fully understood that it would be pointless to assume the role of tsar without their support, and it is only assumed that Nicholas did not fully comprehend at the time. He did not understand that his abdication was to be the end of the Romanov empire.

His abdication was imminent as his ministers reached a point of total dissatisfaction with him. Not only this, but also the disappointment of most of the people he was meant to lead was clear. The mass hysteria and rebellion against the government by the Russian people who had risen to voice their objections was notable. They were tired of the continued suffering, and of being poorly compensated for their work. The shortages of food and land, including basic essential services, were not being met. All of this had devastating consequences such as the numerous deaths of family members who fought in a war they did not support.

Abdication was not an easy process as Nicholas initially resisted it, but he realized he had no choice. Once the revolutionaries had gained control of Petrograd, there was no looking back. Any form of escape was not even considered by either Alexandra or Nicholas as by that stage they were apart and were determined to be together as they knew they were defeated. It has been often said that the week that Nicholas spent traveling to be with his family would likely have been his last attempt at a successful escape from the country.

Russia in Transition

It did not take long for the Provisional Government to be overthrown by the Bolsheviks led by Vladimir Lenin. By the spring of 1918, Russia was in a full-fledged civil war.

When the Treaty of Brest-Litovsk was agreed to on March 3, 1918, it was greeted with utter dismay and shock by both Nicholas and Alexandra that Russia would agree to surrender Ukraine, a large portion of Belarus, the Crimea, Poland, Finland, three Baltic states, and a number of smaller areas that made up a great deal of Russian territory to Germany. Eleven nations would become independent both in Eastern Europe and Western Asia. It also meant that Russia would renege on its agreements with the Allies.

This treaty, however, was annulled on November 11, 1918 when Germany finally surrendered to the Allies.

Russia became the world's first communist state under the leadership of Lenin and one that would eventually become a global superpower. The battles were fierce between the Red Army, who were the Bolsheviks, and the White Army, who were the force wanting to reinstate, or at the very least, rescue the tsar and his family. Not only this but also to gain ultimate power over Russia. There was huge opposition to the Red Army, and the civil war between these two opposing sides was brutal. This three-year battle also saw Lenin nationalize all industry in Russia and plunder the stocks of farmers to feed his troops. He formed new monetary policies that fell under the title of "war communism" that were purely to aid in his quest to defeat the White Army.

The agricultural and manufacturing industries collapsed under the pressures, and it is reckoned that in 1921, the death of five million Russians occurred due to famine and poverty.

There was tremendous resistance to the Soviet government, and Lenin was forced to institute the New Economic Policy as a way to ease the pressures of war communism policies.

The Exile of the Romanovs

Alexandra and the family were initially permitted to remain at Alexander Palace at Tsarskoye Selo under house arrest and with heavily guarded forces under the command of

Prince Lvov while their fate was determined. Nicholas, who at the time was at Mogilev army headquarters, joined them shortly thereafter. Their staff was permitted to remain if they chose to, and other than not being allowed outside the palace and their movements being strictly regulated within the confines of the palace, not too much changed. They lived in relative comfort and were undisturbed and left to their own devices. The family spent much time together, walking, studying, exercising, and even being permitted to attend religious services in the town church.

It was becoming clear that the Provisional Government was increasingly concerned about the threat of being overtaken by the Bolsheviks, so a decision was made to move the tsar and his family to a presumably safer location. It was decided to move them to Tobolsk in Western Siberia on August 13. This decision was made as Tobolsk was rather remote, and it took four days by train and then two ferry crossings to reach their destination by August 19. The family lived in the previous governor's mansion and were not short of comfort by any means, but this was to be short-lived. In October, the Bolsheviks overturned the Provisional Government. At the time, Nicholas was not too concerned and completely underestimated Lenin's influence.

Mounting battles and more violence ensued with the Red Army deciding that the tsar and his family would need to be moved yet again to prevent any attempts to obtain any assistance, rescue, or support. In April 1918 the Bolsheviks relocated them from Western Siberia to remote Yekaterinburg in the Ural Mountains to Ipatiev House. This was ostensibly done for them to await a public trial. In the meanwhile, plans were being made by various sectors for rescue attempts. Even Maria, Rasputin's daughter, and Boris Soloviev, Rasputin's successor, tried to coordinate a rescue with the contacts they had within the monarchy, but it came to naught. Rumors also surfaced of Soloviev's allegiance to both the Germans and the Bolsheviks. When Nikolia Yevgenyevich Markov, the leader of the Union of Russian People and an anti-Bolshevik stalwart, tried to organize a rescue, he was stumped by the uselessness of Soloviev's participation.

Nicholas seemed oblivious to the power Lenin had and the impending danger both he and his family were in. In Ipatiev House, their living conditions started to drastically change. Their hours spent walking were greatly reduced, and the soldiers in charge grew more assertive with the family, even requiring Nicholas to refrain from wearing his uniform and not returning his salute to them. Their previous allowance of being able to attend church services was now denied.

By March 1, the budget that had been allocated to care for the family was reduced dramatically, forcing the family to relinquish some luxuries that they were accustomed to. On March 26, the situation in Tobolsk took a dramatic turn with the Councils of People's Commissars agreeing to the appointment of their own commissar or what would be known today as a mayor. This transpired due to a protest by the soldiers being unpaid and disagreements between the factions who sent representatives to Moscow to state their grievances.

Finally, the depravity of their situation came to a full realization, and the family attempted to send as many messages as they could to anyone, in particular pro-monarchist groups and others that they could think of who may be supportive of their plight. In desperation, Nicholas pleaded with Britain on the connection that his wife was the granddaughter of Queen Victoria, but their request fell upon deaf ears. Upon approaching King George V, who was Nicholas's first cousin and even was known that they looked alike, it looked promising with the offer for refuge in England, but this was withdrawn. It is not clear exactly what happened and why the offer was withdrawn, but there are a few theories. King George V's son the Duke of Windsor stated that his father had decided to personally fetch Nicholas via a ship but was blocked. It is not clear how or who blocked it. Some stories have led others to believe it was King George himself who blocked the impending trip. There were, of course, fears of some type of retaliation in response to anyone who decided to give the tsar and his family refuge as they were in the midst of a war. Sir George William Buchanan, who was the ambassador to Russia at the time, refuted the story that it was King George who reneged on his promise and insisted that it was the Russians who were instrumental in the decision. Years later Buchanan's daughter Meriel penned a book called *The Dissolution of an Empire* and stated that her father wanted to write in his own memoir that the offer was, in fact, withdrawn, but he was prevented from doing so due to the Official Secrets Act. He also had the threat of his pension being withdrawn. It was a smart cover-up that was decided on the premise that if they had given the Romanov family refuge in England, it would not have fared well in the public eye and might have resulted in support of their own monarchy being undermined. The British people viewed the tsar poorly, and the term "Bloody Nicholas" would likely have caused more trouble and possible instability to the monarchy of Britain. It certainly was a case of blood not being thicker than water, and the alliance was not as strong as they thought it was. It is thought that no matter what George had decided, the likelihood of the Bolsheviks releasing the family was probably zero anyway.

Historians who have researched this era extensively are of the opinion that it was in fear of political consequential damage to their own countries that resulted in many of them acting in cowardice by not stepping forward to offer any assistance to the Romanov family. Nicholas also attempted to convince France to help, but they refused. There was too much at stake for both countries to take pity on them that could negatively affect them in retaliation for their assistance. The Romanovs were not popular, and it seemed that they were untouchable for fear of ramifications upon those that were sympathizers. The Romanovs were firmly in the grip of their enemies.

Vasily Yakovlev, a seasoned Bolshevik supporter, was placed as commissar, a title given to those who were effective and influential leaders whose role was to inform, and ultimately convince, the public of communist political information that aligned with their philosophy. In essence, indoctrination of their agenda. Yakovlev swiftly assumed his powerful role and instituted more restrictions upon the Romanov family upon his arrival. He instructed Eugene Kobylinksy, who was the Russian military officer who supervised the imprisonment of the family, that Nicholas was to be relocated to Yekaterinburg. It was a far journey, and Alexei, who was unwell, had to remain behind with two of his sisters. They would only join the rest of the family when he had recovered enough to be able to travel. It was a sad farewell to leave three of the children behind, but they had no choice in the matter. Nicholas, Alexandra and Maria set off the following day on the difficult journey that took two days and included river crossings and numerous changes of horses. They were quite an entourage of 19 carriages! An unsuccessful attempt by the Red Army to capture and murder them was thwarted by these constant changes. Eventually, it was agreed by telegram from Moscow that the family should be transferred to Omsk to ensure their safety and to ostensibly prevent any further attacks on their entourage. This sudden change in plan was mistakenly assumed by the leaders of Yekaterinburg to assume Yakovlev was a traitor and was attempting to allow the family to escape. Nearly 2,000 armed men were deployed to arrest them all! Upon the arrival of the armed men, chaos reigned until finally an impasse was reached from telegrams sent back and forth to Moscow that settled the dispute, and the journey to Yekaterinburg was back on track.

When they arrived on April 30, the family was imprisoned in the two-story home of Nikolay Nikolayevich Ipatiev, which was called Ipatiev House. The conditions worsened further for the family, and even stricter protocols were enforced upon them. Their possessions were greatly reduced, and they were searched relentlessly to ensure they had not smuggled in any luxury items. Many possessions were 'claimed' by the guards.

About a month later the rest of the family arrived, so at least Nicholas, Alexandra, Olga, Tatiana, Maria, Anastasia, and Alexei were all united once more. A tall fence was built around the house to prevent escape or prying eyes, and the house was now called "The House of Special Purpose." The staff complement who volunteered to stay with the family had dwindled down to only three servants and the family doctor, who all lived on the top floor together. The other parts of the house were occupied by guards. The circumstances were dire, and they could only hold on to the hope of a possible rescue and escape.

The country was in continuous turmoil, with executions of reactionaries. News reached them of the murder of Nicholas's brother Michael on June 13. The seriousness of their situation was glaringly obvious. The military state of affairs continued to deteriorate, and the family must have held on to hope that the Bolshevik leaders in Moscow still intended to bring Nicholas to trial.

They were tightly in the grip of the newly-formed revolutionary government, and their fate was doomed. When the White Army gained ground and made significant progress to Yekaterinburg, hoping to rescue the family, the decision was made in a secret meeting of the Yekaterinburg Soviets to assassinate the family. This document that ordered their murder has never surfaced.

Yakov Yurovksy, known to be the chief executioner of the Romanov family, attended to assembling the firing squad and awaited orders to proceed.

Why Were the Romanovs Not Sent to South Russia?

An investigation into the assassination was led by Nikolai Sokolov, a lawyer who was instructed by the White Army's Admiral Alexander Kolchak in February 1919, the year following the horrific the murders. Sokolov was deeply committed to Russia and did not support the Bolsheviks.

During this investigation, to escape the wrath of the Bolsheviks, he had to flee Russia. He was assisted by the commander of the Czechoslovakian Legion and Marice Juan, a French general. Sokolov, fortunately, managed to keep all the investigational evidence with him while he fled, and he continued his research until his death when he succumbed to a heart attack at the age of 42.

During his investigation, Sokolov questioned Alexander Kerensky, who was a lawyer and leader of the Russian Provisional Government at the time. Kerensky was the person who decided where the family was sent initially. South Russia was a safe haven for royalists that had sought safety there, which seemed to be the obvious choice, but of course, this is not where they ended up! The reason stated by Kerensky to send them to Siberia was that due to the heightened and violent state the country was in, it was deemed as far too risky to send them south. It seemed a foolish answer as the areas on the journey they took to get to Siberia were also suffering great moments of unrest. The only valid reason why they were sent to Siberia in Sokolov's opinion was that the royal family was to be subjected to the harshest and most extreme conditions that could be mustered. In a sense, a payback for all the many people the tsar himself had banished to the very same area.

Kerensky was a staunch defender of revolutionary activism and was known to defend many cases. He was part of a committee that assisted the people affected by the Bloody Sunday massacre. His appointment as minister of war in 1917 led to his eventual position as prime minister. He was a charismatic man and was popular among his peers. He was the one who stepped up to ensure the tsarist ministers who were captured were detained as "prisoners of the revolution," which protected them from being thrown into the rioting crowds where they would surely have suffered a dismal fate. Once the Bolsheviks took control of the country, he switched sides quite rapidly, calling for the preservation of the state whereas that was not his view before. Coming up against Lenin was futile, and any chance of a constitutional democracy was wishful thinking. He eventually lived in exile mostly in Britain but also in Paris, Australia, and the United States. Kerensky died in New York, succumbing to cancer, and was one of the last known fundamental members of the Russian Revolution of 1917. He was not popular with Russians who lived abroad and was viewed as integral in the ruin of Russia.

This still begs the question as to why they were not sent South and what the reason behind Kerensky's decision was despite the obvious one of aiming to make the family suffer the same dreary fate the tsar had enforced on many others previously.

Chapter 8:

The Assassination and Bloody Massacre of the Last Romanovs

The initial plan was that the family was to be exiled to England, but this, of course, did not happen. Instead, they ended up in Tobolsk, Yekaterinburg, which was situated in Western Siberia in 1918. Any attempts at a rescue by sympathizers, or the thought of the presence of White Russian Forces, who were against the Bolsheviks, were immediately thwarted by the Red Army.

In Yekaterinburg on July 16, 1918, Yakov Yurovsky received his orders from the Bolsheviks to assassinate the entire family and their servants. Nicholas II of Russia and his wife, Alexandra Fyodorovna, and their five children Olga, Tatiana, Maria, Anastasia, and Alexei. Additionally, their loyal attendants during the imprisonment suffered the same fate. These people were their doctor Eugene Botkin, lady-in-waiting to Alexandra Anna Demidova, Nicholas's head footman Aloise "Alexei" Yegorovich Trupp, and head cook Ivan Kharitonov. The White Army was making good headway, and their arrival was imminent, making the

Bolsheviks nervous that their prisoners potentially could be rescued and taken out of the country. The orders received have many historians agreeing that no order would have been given of this nature without the ultimate approval of Lenin.

The end came to the more than 300-year-old Romanov dynasty quite suddenly and was a brutally dramatic finale. There have been many versions of what took place and filtering through research and finding the most factual was quite a challenge.

Rumors filtered throughout the years post this dramatic turn of events that Nicholas's daughter Anastasia managed to escape and lived, but in 2007, a DNA analysis confirmed remains that were found were indeed hers.

There has been some dispute if the actual date of the assassination was July 16 or 17 or if it was during the night or in the early hours of the morning. Most research indicates that the correct date was July 17, 1918, and that the tragic event took place at night. Nicholas had Alexei in his arms and requested chairs to be brought for him and his wife. Once these chairs were brought in and Nicholas and his wife were seated, Yurovsky announced that it had been decreed that they are all to be executed.

Who Was the Man in Charge of the Assassination?

The man in charge of the assassination, Yurovsky, was a dedicated and committed follower of the Bolsheviks, and in documents researched, he never seemed to have shown an inkling of regret for what he was commanded to do. He recorded in his own notes that the members of the family that did not succumb to bullets were stabbed repeatedly with knives and bayonets. The "House of Special Purpose" indeed had captured this violent man's interpretation of what his duties were with him assuming the role of the one to shoot Nicholas. Yurovsky firmly believed that what he was ordered to do was aid in the betterment of regular Russian people's lives.

He was born into a struggling Jewish family near Tomsk, and he was the eighth child of ten brothers and sisters. He started work as a watchmaker's apprentice and moved around from job to job as a bit of a drifter who had not found his purpose. Coming from a poverty-stricken background and understanding how hard it was to make a living, he rapidly became involved with revolutionary activities. After spending many years in exile, when the 1917 Revolution struck, he was very supportive and was based in Yekaterinburg. As a stalwart supporter of the revolutionary movement, he did everything that was asked (or ordered) of him. His position as commander of the "House of Special Purpose" was a great honor, and he was perfectly appointed to ensure the Romanov family experienced harsh conditions. He was a man of duty and would not tolerate any insolence, both from his prisoners and his guards that served underneath him. A story of him stopping his guards from stealing their prisoners' food is a popular one. Not to say that he was a sympathizer at all. He had scathing views of the Romanovs and was quite insulting about them in his memoirs many years later. But, he never showed any remorse, even for murdering the children. Yurovsky and the other soldiers that were involved in the assassination had to get themselves out of the city very quickly with the impending onslaught from the White Army. Only when the Bolsheviks were victorious in their defeat of the White Army in 1922 did Yurovsky return to Yekaterinburg, where he continued to serve diligently but was not aligned with any further orders of other executions. In 1938, Yurovsky died of a peptic ulcer. One can imagine that supposedly the events of his involvement in the assassinations may have been the cause of an ulcer that is known to be aggravated by stress.

The Massacre

Many versions have been published on assumption of how these unfortunate events unfolded. Assembling well-researched evidence from reputable sources, the section presents what is imagined to have transpired. However, sadly no one will ever know exactly how it all unfolded. What is known is that it was utterly brutal, and their suffering was long and extreme.

The family was woken up in the early hours and required to dress quickly. One can only imagine the panic and the fear as the only clear thing would be the uncertainty of what was going to happen next. Forced downstairs on the ruse that this was for their safety, the family found themselves in a room at the rear of the house. In addition to the family all being hastened to this room, the family doctor and three servants were with them. Little did any of them know what was to come next. Armed Bolshevik police entered the room, and then Yurovsky read out an order that they were to be executed.

Disbelief and shock only could have been the family's response, whereby Yurovsky repeated the order and instructed the executioners to begin shooting. Nicholas was shot several times in the chest, and it is assumed he died shortly after. Alexandra was shot in the head and is believed to be the only one who died instantly. The four daughters were unfortunate as the shower of bullets that were aimed at them prolonged their ultimate deaths due to the many gemstones and diamonds that had been sewn into their clothes that prevented the bullets from penetrating them. This load of wealth was meant to be their bounty to pay for an impending rescue. Their bodies were punctured multiple times with bayonets, and finally, they were all shot in the head. There are other stories that they did not have any jewels sewn into their clothing, but this could also have been part of a cover-up as these jewels were never recovered.

This devastation all took place inside a room, and the air would have been thick with gun smoke, just to add to the chaos of multiple shooters and bodies. A most dreadful and ghastly picture to even imagine the aftermath, never mind the panic and terror during the continuous shooting and violent stabbing. It was a gruesome and unbelievably shocking series of events. Scientific research, many years later shows that their deaths were slow and painful with not only the effects of being shot but also from being stabbed multiple times until their last dying breath.

Disposal of the bodies was rushed and seemed to be ill-planned, which makes one wonder about the series of events that took place when the order was given to execute the family. After the family's possessions and clothing were stripped of any value that they had hidden, they were confiscated by the guards, and where these jewels ended up remains a mystery still today.

Again there are a number of stories of the sequence of events of what happened to their bodies from being mutilated and partially burnt, having acid thrown over their bodies, and then unceremoniously tossing them into a shallow grave to being disposed of outside the city boundaries in a deep mine. The grave that was dug was apparently not deep enough so the next step they took was to try and make the mine cave-in by blowing it up with grenades! The grenades failed to make the mine collapse, which led to a panicked state of affairs to find another suitable grave site to bury the family. There are further stories about the inclement weather playing a negative role in the sequence of events to dispose of their bodies. Finally, another grave site was found, and the family and their servants were eventually buried in two separate graves. The mind just boggles at the chaos and total disrespect for the dead.

The Bolsheviks' Secret

The Bolsheviks did not want it known that the family had been assassinated and kept it a secret. The death of Nicholas only was released to the public via a publication in the Bolshevik's official party newspaper. The deaths of the rest of his family were secret and created a series of rumors arising around the mystery. It seemed that it was mostly accepted that the rest of the family were still alive and were moved to a secret location for their security.

In the ensuing 84 days, a further 27 deaths by assassination were conducted by the Bolsheviks of the tsar's relatives and allies with the modus operandi to wipe out any connections to them. Many of these people's bodies were never to be found being either burnt so badly that they could not be identified or they were just dumped in mass graves. The reasons for the secrecy can be speculated among many different versions including fear of reprisal of George V that could easily have toppled the Bolsheviks' teetering government as there were many disputes.

The White Army tried to capitalize on the rumors to stir up distrust for Lenin and create distrust for the Bolshevik movement. Many have assumed that it was Lenin who gave the final order for the dreadful assassination, but it has come to light that he was in fact supportive of a public trial, and it was Leon Trotsky who gave the ultimate order. Lenin did not want the truth revealed that the whole family had been assassinated as this would have harmed his campaign, and he would have been to blame. He was satisfied with the theories and rumors that were bandied about, taking the focus off him and the Bolshevik rule. Rather the focus was on manhunts and planned rescue for the remaining family than targeting his objectives. It was a massively cowardly choice.

Discoveries in Later Years

In 1919 the Bolsheviks claimed that the family had been murdered by socialist revolutionaries then turned about-face in 1922 with firm denial about their deaths. It was only in 1926 that the Soviet government admitted to the murders of the family due to exposure in a French publication. They vehemently denied Lenin was involved in any way. There were multiple Romanov imposters throughout the succeeding years just to add to more confusion and growing mystery about the family. A Soviet Union official stated that the Romanov family and entourage were assassinated by a firing squad under orders received from the Ural Regional Soviet. Historical research leans heavily on the order being given by the Moscow government, in particular from Lenin and Yakov Sverdlov, who was an influential member of the Russian Social Democratic Party and worked closely with Lenin. Neither of them wanted the family rescued by the White Army and making them look weak. Leon Trotsky's memoirs support this theory. To date, there has been no written record of any order that has surfaced, and nothing will likely surface in the future. It cannot be denied that no matter who gave the order, those that are considered guilty of this horrific historical saga supported it in some way.

It was only in 1979 that the bodies of Nicholas, Alexandra, and three of their daughters were found. The doctor and the three servants' bodies were among the discoveries of archaeologist Alexander Avdonin. It took the Soviet Union until 1989 to acknowledge this discovery. The bodies were only dug up in 1998 when they were officially identified using forensic testing with the assistance of British DNA experts. They conclusively identified four males and five females of which a father and a mother were identified and three daughters. The other four remains were thought to be servants, thus the mystery of Alexei and Anastasia surfaced—where were they?

The remains were interred at St. Petersburg Cathedral in 1998, and a state funeral was held. It was a very solemn event that was televised nationwide to demonstrate Russia's reconciliation with its past history. The coffins were paraded down a red carpet flanked by soldiers in dress uniforms as a mark of respect. The message presented by President Boris Yeltsin, who was a Communist Party leader, was that never again should political change by violence be repeated like this travesty. Some are of the thinking that as this event was assembled by Yeltsin, it was just a show of a big political move mostly to indicate Russia's strategy to show the world their intention to promote a free and democratic Russia. It was glaringly prudent that the superior of the Orthodox Church of that time was absent. However, there was representation from other priests of the revived Russian Orthodox Church who gave their blessings to the departed.

In 2007, a further discovery of bones near Yekaterinburg was unearthed in a smaller grave near where the rest of the family were located. DNA testing established that these bones were most certainly Alexei and his sister Anastasia. It took until October 1, 2008 after much persuasion for the Supreme Court of Russia to pass a ruling that Nicholas and his entire family suffered political mistreatment. There could be no persecution thereafter though as all the alleged perpetrators had since died.

Finally, and quite shockingly, in 2015 with much intervention from the Russian Orthodox Church, who were doubtful of the confirmation that the bodies found were indeed the family, they insisted the bodies of Nicholas and Alexandra be exhumed for further DNA testing to be performed. It was again confirmed in 2018 that it was most certainly their bodies.

The remains of the two siblings that were found after the final burial of the family in St. Petersburg Cathedral still are being kept in a Russian state archive. Whether or not they will be buried at some stage with the rest of the family remains unclear.

Ongoing Mysteries and Tales

There has always been the ongoing mystery about Anastasia's death and also Alexei, whose remains were not discovered at the original burial site. In 1928 a young woman who looked to be the same age as Anastasia would have been stated that she was the Grand Duchess Anastasia, going by the name Anastasia Tschaikovsky or Anna Anderson. She arrived in New York City and held a press briefing where she said she was there to have surgery done on her jaw that had been broken when she escaped the brutal attack on her family. She claimed she had been hit in the face by a Bolshevik soldier in July 1918. Gleb Botkin, who was the son of the Romanov's family doctor who also was executed that fatal night and even called her "Your Highness" was convinced of her claim. They had played together as children, and he said he had no doubt it was her.

Prior to this, she was rescued from the Landwehr Canal in Berlin in 1920. She initially did not want to say who she was and was committed to a mental asylum in Dalldorf. Two years went by and then in 1922, she suddenly claimed she was the Grand Duchess Anastasia. She created quite a stir with many supporters who felt sympathy towards her, particularly upon hearing about how scarred her body was. She said these scars were from the wounds inflicted by the Bolshevik soldiers, but that there was one soldier that helped her escape once he realized she was still alive after the attack. She was eventually released from the mental asylum and ended up living with one of the many supporters of her claim. She spent a great deal of time with relatives of the Romanovs as they wanted to know if it was indeed true. There were some that were very doubtful of her claims as she had no recollection of some of the memorable events in the family's day-to-day life. Her lack of being able to speak languages, such as French, Russian, and English, that Anastasia was fluent in was also puzzling but was dismissed due to her mental instability. She was readmitted to the mental institution numerous times over the years suffering from mental breakdowns.

She had a horde of supporters and a 30-year battle ensued whereby the attempt to claim her fortune and title was waged. Eventually, in 1970 a German court threw out her case as it could not be proven that she was even related to the Romanovs. There were theories that she was a mentally disturbed woman called Franziska Schanzkowska that was unearthed by an investigation that was launched by the Grand Duke of Hesse. He was the brother of Alexandra and Anastasia's uncle. He was not a supporter of her claim and was determined to prove it. Schanzkowska was a Polish-German woman who worked in factories and had a long history of mental instability. Her scars were apparently from an explosion that happened in the factory in 1916. None of this was proven. In 1968 she married a history professor and settled in the United States and passed away in 1984.

There were many women, more than 100, who surfaced between the years 1918 and 1928 with the very same claim but all came to nothing. Eventually, the remainder of the Romanov estate was awarded to the Duchess of Mecklenburg.

What Happened to the Russian Crown Jewels?

Another mystery! There was a massive dispute amongst the Bolsheviks who wanted the jewels as they needed money to fund their motives. Some had the view of these jewels being a symbol of oppression by the monarchy and should be sold to benefit the working class of Russia. Fortunately, the historical value and significance were recognized and the crown jewels (or many of them!) were safely kept. Today most of them are kept in the Kremlin museums.

The collection of the Romanov jewels was quite substantial and included numerous necklaces, rings, intricate crowns, brooches, jeweled scepters, medals, and many other elaborate bejeweled pieces. There are documented journals of what the collection in its entirety contains that were compiled in the 1920s by the Soviet Union. The collection of jewels had been collected since 1613 and passed along to the Romanov family throughout the years until 1917. There have been some discrepancies in the records made of the collection of jewels with four pieces missing in 1925. One of these appeared at a Christie's auction so that leaves three extremely valuable items still somewhere out there. It does make one ponder about where they are, and if they will ever surface, never mind their value in today's terms.

Conclusion

It is clear that Nicholas II and his family were not popular with most of the Russian population for a great deal of time even before the Bolsheviks took control in 1918. The autocratic status and way of life were so far removed from the general man on the street of Russia whose suffering continued to worsen during the Romanov reign, and this is what bred bitterness and discontent towards the monarchy. His continuous indecisiveness and self-doubt may have been his ultimate downfall. Russia was an enormous country that added to the difficulties of ruling effectively. A country can only be as strong as their leader is.

Nicholas was absolutely devoted to his wife and his family but lacked the abilities that a leader needed to rule successfully and gain respect. Even though his efforts in the construction of the Trans-Siberian Railroad were done with good intentions, it led to a catastrophic war and caused immense suffering for his country.

Since 1905 trouble had been brewing against the aristocracy and the growth of revolutionary uprisings and rebel groups were becoming more organized. Nicholas was to be the ultimate example of what unfolds when misguided advice is taken, and what it would lead to. He was so far removed from what his people needed as he was brought up in a system that was so outdated and behind the times. Progress was only for the wealthy and the masses were becoming fed up. The government's way of ruling was not efficient and created more problems for the poor than solutions.

Nicholas made a disastrous choice to remove the current and popular commander of his army and assume the role himself. The expectations of him to win battles for Russia were very high, and even though he had military training, he was nowhere near competent to lead an entire army into battle. His numerous defeats and poor planning and control led to more discontent among his people who viewed him as a failed leader who was not able to bring the victory home. His own military did not trust him, and how could they when he was such a poor example of a leader who was responsible for the many deaths of their fellow men. Not only this, but the indignity felt by the men who fought in the battles and had to deal with coping with devastating losses to the Japanese and the Germans just fueled the utter disrespect for him.

The family had such absolute blind faith in Rasputin no matter that he was viewed by most as being a scandalous cretin. He tricked them into believing him and his presumed special powers. Aside from being the one healer who managed to help their son, it was his interference with the governing of Russia that should have been stopped immediately by Nicholas. When Nicholas was away at war and Alexandra was acting in his place to rule Russia in his absence, she was dismal at the job, which infuriated much of Russia. Rasputin had so much influence over her, and she was tenfold more ineffective at leading the country than he was. Nicholas was viewed in a very poor light as having no control over the power Rasputin had over his family and, in particular, over his wife and did nothing about it. The death of Rasputin opened up the pathway to the demise of the Romanovs, but certainly, the aristocrats never imagined it would end in the way it finally did.

It could be viewed that the legacy of Nicholas stemmed from the Russian Revolution, and all the other events that followed in its wake were the result of a leader that could not adapt to how the world and his country, in particular, were changing. His inability to adjust his way of thinking was so dogmatic due to his upbringing, which left little room for him to actually change his views and way of ruling, even if he wanted to. It was almost as if he had no idea how to, so he just continued in the same manner. The calls for a republic and constitution and the preservation of the monarchy were in contradiction with each other. The ultimate outcome of Russia becoming a communist state was inevitable.

The October Manifesto was meant to be a victory for the working class of Russia, but it only led to disappointment again in their tsar who kept dissolving the Duma to suit his own objectives. In today's terms, it would be coined as 'lip-service' to the people.

The aftermath of the Bloody Sunday disaster in 1905 earned him the title "Nicholas the Bloody" and turned the masses against him with his poor handling of the outcome of the countless and avoidable deaths that occurred. His attendance of a ball that was held at the French Embassy on the evening of the event left a very sour taste among many. This probably was the final call for many of his supporters to change their views and look for alternatives for a leader to lead them. Hindsight is the perfect science, but the advice he took to continue with the celebrations when so many of his fellow men were suffering was such a stupid thing to do.

Between 1916 to 1917 was a terrible time in Russia with a massive food crisis across the country with many people suffering from starvation. The strikes and riots that broke out did little to change their situation. The people of Russia were hungry and sick, and they viewed the tsar as being so out of touch with their situation as he was oblivious to how it was to be in their position. His life did not seem at all affected during this terrible time of food shortages. They expected him to solve the problems and be their leader who had the power to affect change efficiently to make their lives better.

Did you enjoy reading a concise version of the rise and fall of Russia's most famous family? There was a lot of information, stories, and tales to craft into this engaging book. While some mystery remains, I hope you learned more about this fascinating family and the challenging times in which they lived.

I would love to hear your thoughts on this book. Please leave a review as it will be much appreciated.

References

Alpha History. (2019, January 13). *The "Bloody Sunday" petition to the tsar (1905)*. Russian Revolution. https://alphahistory.com/russianrevolution/ bloody-sunday-petition-1905/

Andreyev, N. (2019). Ivan the Terrible | Biography, achievements, & facts. In *Encyclopædia Britannica*. https://www.britannica.com/biography/ Ivan-the-Terrible

Astanina, A., & RBTH. (2015, April 18). *Nikolai Sokolov: The man who revealed the story of the Romanov killings*. Russia Beyond. https://www.rbth.com/arts/2015/04/18/nikolai_s okolov_the_man_who_revealed_the_story_of_the_ romanov_killings_45299.html

Advantour. (2001). *Troubles in Russia (1598 – 1613). History of Russia.* Www.advantour.com. https://www.advantor.com/russia/history/time-of-troubles.htm

BBC. (2014). *Catherine the Great*. https://www.bbc.co.uk/history/historic_figures/ca therine_the_great.shtml

BBC. (2022). *The Russification of national minorities - Imperial Russia - Government and People - National 5 History Revision*.

https://www.bbc.co.uk/bitesize/guides/z6rjy9q/re
vision/7

Bilyeau, N. (2020, March 21). Could the British royal family
have saved the Romanovs? *Town & Country*.
https://www.townandcountrymag.com/society/tra
dition/   a31028924/windsors-romanovs-
relationship-last-gathering-true-story/

Biography.com Editors. (2015, May 19). *Nicholas II.*
https://www.biography.com/royalty/nicholas-ii

Brainard, J. (2020). *World History: Russia: Rasputin.*
Historywiz.com.
https://www.historywiz.com/historymakers/rasput
in.htm

Britannica. (2019). Alexandra | Biography, death, & facts.
In   *Encyclopædia*   *Britannica.*
https://www.britannica.com/biography/Alexandra
-empress-consort-of-Russia

Britannica. (2019). Boyar | Russian aristocrat. In
Encyclopædia   *Britannica.*
https://www.britannica.com/topic/boyar

Britannica. (2019). Emancipation Manifesto | Russia
[1861].   In   *Encyclopedia*   *Brittanica*
https://www.britannica.com/event/Emancipation-
Manifesto

Britannica. (2019). Russian Revolution of 1905. In
Encyclopædia   *Britannica.*
https://www.britannica.com/event/Russian-
Revolution-of-1905

Britannica. (2019). Romanov dynasty | Definition, history, significance, & facts. In *Encyclopædia Britannica.* https://www.britannica.com/topic/Romanov-dynasty

Brittanica. (2021). *Understand the causes and the effects of the Russo-Japanese War.* In *Encyclopædia Britannica* https://www.britannica.com/ summary/Russo-Japanese-War

Britannica. (2022). Alexander II | Legacy. In *Encyclopedia Britannica.* https://www.britannica.com/biography/Alexander-II-emperor-of-Russia/Legacy

Cano, R. (2021, May 13). *This is why the Bolsheviks concealed the cowardly murder of the Czar royal family.* We Are the Mighty. https://www.wearethemighty.com/mighty-history/why-the-bolsheviks-murdered-royals/

Cavendish, R. (2005). *"Bloody Sunday" in St Petersburg.* Www.historytoday.com. https://www.historytoday.com/archive/months-past/bloody-sunday-st-petersburg

Choi, D. (2020, June 3). *When a Japanese man almost assassinated the last tsar of Russia.* Medium. https://historyofyesterday.com/when-a-japanese-man- almost-assassinated-the-last-tsar-of-russia-3ab71237ee02

Constitutional Rights Foundation. (2022). The riddle of the Romanovs. https://www.crf-usa.org/bill-of-rights-in-action/bria-13-3-a-the-riddle-of-the-romanovs

Daniels, P. (2012, August 28). *Czar Nicholas II*. ThoughtCo. https://www.thoughtco.com/nicholas-ii-1779830

Dukes, P. (2016). *Remembering Russia's great war*. Historytoday.com. https://www.historytoday.com/remembering-russia%E2%80%99s-great-war

Gilbert, P. (2021, February 7). *On this day in 1919: Nikolai Sokolov launched his investigation into the deaths of the Imperial Family*. Nicholas II. https://tsarnicholas.org/2021/02/07/on-this-day-in-1919-nikolai-sokolov-launched-his-investigation-into-the-deaths-of-the-imperial-family/

Greenspan, J. (2018, August 23). *Why Peter the Great tortured and killed his own son*. HISTORY. https://www.history.com/news/peter-the-great-tortured-killed-own-son

Harris, C. (2016, December 27). The murder of Rasputin, 100 years later. *Smithsonian Magazine*. https://www.smithsonianmag.com/history/murder-rasputin-100- years-later-180961572/

Heichelbech, R. (2020, August 7). *What ever happened to the crown jewels of the Romanov family?* Dusty Old Thing. https://dustyoldthing.com/romanov-crown-jewels/

History.com Editors. (2019, March 12). *Czar Alexander II assassinated in St. Petersburg*. HISTORY. https://www.history.com/this-day-in-history/ czar-alexander-ii-assassinated

History.com Editors. (2019). *Did any of the Romanovs survive?* HISTORY. https://www.history.com/news/did-any-of-the-romanovs-survive

History.com Editors. (2010, February 9). *Woman claiming to be Anastasia Romanov arrives in the U.S.* HISTORY. https://www.history.com/ this-day-in-history/anastasia-arrives-in-the-united-states

History.com Editors. (2009, October 29). *World War I.* HISTORY. https://www.history.com/topics/world-war-i/world-war-i-history

History.com Editors. (2020). *Vladimir Lenin.* HISTORY. https://www.history.com/topics/russia/vladimir-lenin#section_5

Jarus, O. (2017, May 23). *Catherine the Great: Biography, accomplishments & death.* Live Science. https://www.livescience.com/42006-catherine-the-great.html

John L.H. Keep. (2019). Nicholas II | Biography, death, & facts. In *Encyclopædia Britannica.* https://www.britannica.com/biography/Nicholas-II-tsar-of-Russia

Kelly, C. (2006, April 1). Review: Catherine the Great by Virginia Rounding. *The Guardian.* https://www.theguardian.com/books/2006/apr/01/ featuresreviews.guardianreview7

Kiger, P. J. (2021, April 6). *8 events that led to World War I.* HISTORY. https://www.history.com/news/world-war-i-causes

Manaev, G. (2020, February 15). *Who voluntarily gave up the Russian throne?* Russia Beyond. https://www.rbth.com/history/331702-who-voluntarily- abdicated-russian-throne

Maranzani, B. (2018, August 23). *8 things you didn't know about Catherine the Great.* HISTORY. https://www.history.com/news/8-things-you-didnt-know- about-catherine-the-great

MNE Today. (2022, June 8). *Princesses Milica and Anastasia of Montenegro - The digital insider to Montenegro.* https://mne.today/post/princess-milica-anastasia-montenegro/

Montefiore, Simon Sebag. (2016). *Romanovs.* Weidenfield & Nicholson.

Montefiore, Simon Sebag. (2016, October 5). The devastating true story of the Romanov family's execution. *Town & Country.* https://www.townandcountrymag.com/society/tradition/a8072/russian-tsar-execution/

National Hemophilia Council. (2015). *Should people with haemophilia avoid aspirin?* http://nationalhaemophiliacouncil.ie/home/faqs/should_people_with_haemophilia_avoid_aspirin/

National Hemophilia Foundation. (2021). *Hemophilia A.*
https://www.hemophilia.org/bleeding-disorders-a-
z/types/hemophilia-a

National Hemophilia Foundation. (2022, March 29). *An
interview with Dr. Helen Rappaport.*
https://www.hemophilia.org/news/hemophilia-in-
the- romanov-family

New World Encyclopedia. (2021). *1905 Russian Revolution.*
In *New World Encyclopedia*
https://www.newworldencyclopedia.org/entry/190
5_Russian_Revolution#Creation_of_Duma_and_St
olypin

New World Encyclopedia. (2022). *Boris Godunov.* In *New
World Encyclopedia*
https://www.newworldencyclopedia.org/entry/Bor
is_Godunov

Nikiforov, L. (2019). Peter I | Biography,
accomplishments, facts, & significance. In
Encyclopædia Britannica.
https://www.britannica.com/biography/ Peter-the-
Great

Office of the Historian. (2016). *The Treaty of Portsmouth and
the Russo-Japanese War, 1904-1905.* U.S. Department
of State.
https://history.state.gov/milestones/1899-
1913/portsmouth-
treaty#:~:text=The%20Treaty%20of%20
Portsmouth%20formally

Ray, M. (2000). *Russian Empire - Revolution of 1905 and the First and Second Dumas.* In *Encyclopedia Britannica.* https://www.britannica.com/place/ Russian-Empire/Revolution-of-1905-and-the-First-and-Second-Dumas

Russiapedia. (2005). Of Russian origin: *Old style and new style*Russiapedia https://russiapedia.rt.com/of-russian-origin/old-style-and-new-style/index.html

Saint-Petersburg.com. (2001). *Biography of Emperor Nicholas I of Russia.* Www.saint-Petersburg.com. http://www.saint-petersburg.com/ royal-family/nicholas-i/

Saint-Petersburg.com. (2019). *Biography of Peter the Great of Russia.* Saint-Petersburg.com. http://www.saint-petersburg.com/royal-family/peter-the-great/

Schimmelpenninck van der Oye, D. (2018). *War aims and war aims discussions (Russian Empire).* In *International Encyclopedia of the First World War (WW1).* https://encyclopedia.1914-1918-online.net/article/war_aims_and_war_aims_discussions_russian_empire

Scully, R. E. (2016, December 22). Three centuries of Romanov rule brought Russia, in fits and starts, toward modernity. *America Magazine.* https://www.americamagazine.org/arts-culture/2016/12/22/three-centuries-romanov-rule-brought-russia-fits-and-starts-toward

Seville, C. (Director). (2017). *The Russian Revolution [Film].* Netflix.

Shlapentokh, D. (2019, May 15). *The Time of Troubles: Did it ever end?* Institute of Modern Russia. https://imrussia.org/en/analysis/3021-the-time-of-trouble-has-it-ever-ended-in-russia

Solly, M. (2020, May 17). The Story of Catherine the Great. *Smithsonian Magazine.* https://www.smithsonianmag.com/history/true-story-catherine-great-180974863/

The New Soviet Child. (2020). *Introduction: Culture, the Romanovs, and the Russian Revolutions.* https://sites.uw.edu/kirschn/home/introduction/

The State Duma. (2011). *History of the State Duma.* http://duma.gov.ru/en/duma/about/history/information/

Timofeychev, A. (2018, October 8). *Why did Britain's King George V betray Russia's last tsar?* Russia Beyond. https://www.rbth.com/history/329281-why-did-king-george-betray-nicholas

Treasures of the world. (1999). *Faberge Eggs - Nicholas and Romanov Russia.* PBS.http://www.pbs.org/treasuresoftheworld/faberge/flevel_1/f1a_nicholas_and_russia.html

Walker, F. A. (1967). Constantine Pavlovich: An Appraisal. *Slavic Review, 26*(3), 445–452. https://doi.org/10.2307/2492727

Walsh, E. (1928, February). The fall of the Russian Empire: The end of the monarchy.. *The Atlantic.* https://www.theatlantic.com/magazine/archive/19

28/02/the-fall-of-the-russian-empire-the-end-of-
the-monarchy/303869/

Watts, C. (1998). *The Reforms of Tsar Alexander II.*
Www.historytoday.com.
https://www.historytoday.com/archive/reforms-
tsar-alexander-ii

Waxman, O. B. (2019, October 21). The real history behind
HBO's "Catherine the Great." *Time.*
https://time.com/5696556/catherine-the-great-
history/

Widener, M. (2012, March 12). *Monuments of Imperial Russian
Law: The Nakaz in*

English | Lillian Goldman Law Library. Library.law.yale.edu.

Yegorov, Oleg. (2017, August 24). *From shaving to potatoes: 5
things that Peter the Great brought to Russia.* Russia
Beyond.
https://www.rbth.com/politics_and_society/2017/
08/24/from-shaving-to-potatoes-5-things-that-
peter-the-great-brought-to-russia_827666

Printed in Great Britain
by Amazon

30851331R00076